Dear Dad,

Happy Birthday !! 11/6/07.

Creative ...   ...oans &
...   ...Late
this mo...   ...before
gird...   ...been

CREATIVE EDITING

a bargain if it just
stimulates your pen any
amount! Check page 204.

carriage

Many happy ^ returns !

Love from one of your

eager readers !

CREATIVE EDITING

Spot what's wrong with your writing before an editor does

MARY MACKIE

VICTOR GOLLANCZ
LONDON

First published in Great Britain simultaneously in
hardback and paperback 1995
by Victor Gollancz
An imprint of the Cassell Group
Wellington House, 125 Strand, London WC2R 0BB

A catalogue record for this book is
available from the British Library.

ISBN 0 575 05985 0 (hb)
ISBN 0 575 06001 8 (pb)

Phototypeset in Great Britain by
Rowland Phototypesetting Ltd, Bury St Edmunds, Suffolk
Printed and bound in Great Britain by
Mackays of Chatham plc, Chatham, Kent

Contents

Acknowledgements

I'm indebted to those students and friends who allowed me free use of their rough, unedited work from which to pick examples. Some of them said it was probably their only chance of getting into print. May they be proved wrong.

My warmest thanks and best wishes to:
Barbara Annison; Jackie Arnett; Mollie Bayfield; Norma Benstead; Cathy Charles; Vivienne Fenge; Les Gaskin; Stephanie Howard; Josie Irving; Eileen Johnson; Gill Lee; Ella Perry; Sue Stevens; Tom Stockwell; Eve Tidman; Karen Treacher; Kit Young;

and my husband, Chris Mackie, to whom go extra thanks and love for being himself.

Do you want to be a writer?

Are you already trying to get into print?

Have you ever wondered why manuscripts you send out come back with a polite 'No, thank you'? Or with maybe just an unhelpful rejection slip? Or don't come back at all?

Would you like to know how to improve your chances?

If you answer 'Yes,' to any of these questions – whether you're a 'wannabee', a trier, or an improver – this book is for you.

About This Book

When I first mooted the possibility of a book on self-editing, a friendly editor commented, 'Something like that is sorely needed. You should see some of the manuscripts that come across my desk!' Having tutored evening classes in creative writing, and having started up three separate writers' groups in different areas of the country, thus seeing my share of hopeful manuscripts, I knew what she meant: too many beginners doom their work to rejection because they send it out looking like Frankenstein's monster, misshapen and badly finished. Such writers don't appear to understand that, in order to create publishable prose, you have to begin by sticking to a few basic rules. Perhaps these innocents cling to the illusion that their eventual editor will correct all faults of structure, style, content, grammar, syntax, spelling . . . Alas, not so. Once you've mastered the nuts and bolts stage, you then have to go further and *work* on your words to get them right, and as a final touch you go over your piece again, adding a veneer of professional polish.

If you're lucky, your editor may point out the odd glaring error in an otherwise acceptable manuscript, but correcting basic flaws is *your* responsibility, part of your job, as a writer. After all, however valuable a diamond may be, when it first sees the light it looks like a lump of worthless quartz. So, having mined your gem from the deeps of your imagination, why display it in its raw state? It's up to you to hone and polish, bring out the hidden beauty and display its dazzling facets, in the hope that some lucky publisher will be tempted to buy.

To quote Alexander Pope: 'True ease in writing comes from art, not chance, As those move easiest who have learned to dance.'

Be wary of any writer who claims never to rewrite a single word. There may be the odd, rare, genius of this kind but, more often, the person who makes such a claim is either a liar or a fool – too lazy to bother, or simply too amateurish to see any faults. All the classic writers wrote and rewrote. If you doubt me, go to the British Museum and look at some of the original drafts the masters have left us, complete with scratching out and scribbled addenda, sometimes so profuse as to obliterate the original words. Beautiful prose and poetry is worked at, shaped and crafted: it does not flow, perfectly formed, straight from the glowing furnace of inspiration.

You and I may not aspire to write Great Literature or Deathless Prose. We're ordinary working writers, trying to produce good, saleable, readable work, which publishers will want to print and the majority of readers will find enjoyable and satisfying. To be a good story-teller, to keep your reader reading, to develop work with the ICPID factor (what makes a reader declare, 'I couldn't put it down!') – that's what we *can* try for.

In the following pages you will find advice on many aspects of writing. We shall touch on the basics of story-telling as we go: plot, character, dialogue, beginnings and endings are all necessary ingredients, as is good English and sturdy structure. All of these find their place here. But my main object is to encourage you to take a fresh, objective look at your own work and see how you might improve it *before* you put it in the post.

Since it's easier to see the mote in someone else's eye than the beam in our own, we shall be studying examples of 'first draft' writing. Some is culled from my own work (early and not so early), others have been contributed by students and friends brave enough to let me use their early drafts as examples to help other struggling beginners. The extracts do not necessarily qualify as 'bad' writing, they're simply rough, unedited work, such as any of us might dash off in the heat of creativity. But they can all be improved, and we're going to look at some ways of doing that.

I am indebted to all who contributed.

Where I've quoted from my own published work I've done so purely for practical reasons: it's readily accessible and I don't need to apply for special permission to use it. Such examples are *not* intended to be taken as the only possible way to tackle these techniques – they simply provide an illustration of *my* methods, honed and polished over thirty-odd years.

At the end of each section you'll find exercises you might like to try. I've included them partly for your amusement but also because only by doing it yourself can you learn the real secrets of writing. Theory is fine but, as they say, practice makes perfect. Well . . . maybe not perfect – none of us is *ever* beyond improvement: let's settle for 'publishable', shall we? That's an attainable goal.

1 · Mining Your Diamond

Anybody can dream up writing ideas. **Many** make a start at putting ideas on paper. **Some** carry on and finish the project. Of those who do so, **a few** manage to get published.

If you find this discouraging, you're not a writer – go away and find some other way of passing the time. I almost put 'earning a living', but the ones who do that are a few of the few, and as for making a fortune . . . only about one per cent of published writers manage that. May you find yourself among that select band some day.

If, on the other hand, you don't care about the obstacles; if you want to write, even if never a word sees print; or if you find the hurdles ahead only tend to spur you on and make you determined to make it in spite of the odds, then – good for you! Welcome to the club.

Writers are born, not made, they say. Born, that is, with what the Roman poet Juvenal called 'the inveterate itch' for putting words on paper or, nowadays, on screen. If you don't have that urge, nothing on earth will persuade you that the time and effort is worthwhile. If you do have it, nothing on earth will prevent you from scratching that itch – not age (Mary Wesley started at seventy); not incapacity (a well-published acquaintance of mine is registered blind but writes with the aid of a huge felt pen and a projector screen); not even family commitments or the needs of marital harmony.

Be warned!

But then, since you're born that way, you may as well enjoy it. Writing should be fun. Samuel Johnson famously said that, 'No man but a blockhead ever wrote, except for money.' But he'll excuse me if I argue: the money, if it comes, is a welcome by-product, but it can't be counted on; some of us write for the sheer love of words. What bliss to sit before an empty page and know you're going to fill it with wonderful thoughts and images.

I lie, of course – that empty page is *terrifying*!

But let's assume you were born with the inveterate itch. You've been scribbling since the age of four, or wanting to, or thinking about trying it. You're overflowing with ideas. You're raring to go. You've read all the 'how-to' books on writing fiction/ prose/poetry/stories/novels/articles/fillers/screenplays/et cetera and so forth. You're attending evening classes; you've joined your local writers' group; you subscribe to one or more of the writers' magazines . . .

These things are useful, interesting, necessary, socially enjoy-able, stimulating, maddening, a waste of time and money – take your pick which fits which. But groups, classes, confer-ences and 'how-to' books – including this one – can only give you clues to the mysteries, pointers along the way. The trick is knowing how best to use the hints and tips you glean from these sources.

You alone can teach yourself that skill. Sooner or later, it's just you and that empty page.

Forget the Muse – she's a fickle jade at best. Remember the saying: *One per cent inspiration, the rest perspiration, dedi-cation, application* . . . Every would-be writer has to stop dreaming at some stage, stop wanting-to-be and actually do it. How do you become a writer? You just *be* a writer. Put words on paper. That's all. Getting published is in the future: first you have to write.

You might make yourself a notice:

> THE **ONLY WAY** TO LEARN
> HOW TO WRITE
> is to sit down
> and do it

Put it near your place of work, and look at it daily.

Here's where the hard work starts.

You did know it was hard work, didn't you?

Methods of writing

Successful writers are often asked exactly *how* they go about writing.

Do they have a quiet study at home? Do they use a rented office? Have they a summerhouse retreat by a river at the bottom of their garden? Or a cottage in the Alps? Maybe they work in a wine bar, or a coffee shop, or on top of a double-decker bus. Do they use a pen, a pencil, or a PC? What colour paper? What size – A4, ruled or plain, or a reporter's notebook?

My husband says that if some best-selling author declared a preference for working in the bathroom, with one foot on the cistern, naked but for pink earmuffs, and using a green pen on striped paper, while listening to Japanese wind instruments on a personal stereo . . . some fool would go away and try to copy the same methods in the belief that emulation would bring the same success. The fact is, methods of writing vary as widely as do writers as people.

Some authors work office hours, nine to five, others go as the mood takes them. Some need solitude; some can work amid bedlam. Some need booze, or cigarettes (or think they do); some are night birds, some rise with the lark. I could go on, but you probably see the point — whatever suits *you* is your best method.

In case you're wondering, my own first forty-odd books were written longhand, in pencil or biro, then painfully typed on a portable machine, with two fingers. I graduated eventually to an electric typewriter and finally, after much resistance, acquired a word processor. Wondrous machine. Wouldn't be without it. Occasionally, if parted from my beloved computer for more than a day or two, I go back to longhand. Or, if I'm stuck in a writer's block, I imagine that handwriting eases the flow. But, when the work eventually goes on screen with the rest, even I can't tell where the seams are. And I'm still a two-finger typist. I haven't had the time to learn proper typing — I've been too busy writing.

So, the advice is — where working methods are concerned, DO YOUR OWN THING. It's *what* you write that matters, not how.

Deciding what to write

Writing has many different avenues and each one calls for a different discipline; poetry, short stories, articles, novels, non-fiction books, plays, films — all require a separate strategy. Do you aim to write for children, teenagers or adults? Is your natural style humorous or more serious? Are you interested in producing romances, westerns, travel guides, science fiction, spy thrillers, hobby subjects, history? These are just a few of the variations, but I point them out to demonstrate how wide is your choice. Your own particular talent may lend itself to only one discipline, or you may cover several, but you must discover for yourself which aspect is best for you.

Many people feel that **poems** are easy because they're short. But that's a fallacy: true poetry is an art form. If you have a facility for rhyming, and if you can make your lines scan without much trouble, the result may well be acceptable verse. But is it poetry? Even free verse, formless as it may look to the uninitiated, has its laws, its inner rhymes, its alliteration, careful choice of words and underlying framework that make it poetry and not just prose chopped up into short lines and set down in a stack on the page. Sadly, the world is full of abysmal verse masquerading as poetry, penned by deluded souls who are not aware that, behind their backs, people are sniggering, 'What awful doggerel!' Far too many amateur scribblers imagine themselves to be poets because friends and family praise them and because the local paper prints their outpourings in the 'Letters' section, or even, heaven help us, in 'Poetry Corner'. Please . . . don't add to this literary pollution. If you like to write verse, do so by all means, but remember that even verse needs editing, polishing, shaping. The Muse who wakes you at three in the morning with a brilliant poem is generally half asleep, just as you are at that hour when you write down the words in a rush of 'inspiration'. So reconsider her words by sombre daylight. With a little help from your skill and knowledge as a wordsmith, they might just turn into real poetry.

Several of my students have come to classes declaring their intention to 'start with **children's stories** and work up to adult stuff'. Actually, it's more the other way round – you graduate *up* to writing for children. Doing it well is extremely difficult;

you need a good grasp of what makes children tick; a facility for using the right kind of language — different for each age group, and *not* full of current slang, which goes in and out of fashion too frequently. Your own grandchildren may love the stories you tell them. But your own grandchildren are not impartial judges. You need to be a highly skilled writer, in tune with the great mass of today's youngsters, in order to be successful as a children's author today.

Neither are **short stories and articles** an easy option simply because they take less time to write. They must be well-crafted, shaped so that every word counts, tailored to express one central idea. The short-short twist-ending story, usually written to around a thousand words, requires especial skill if it's to be done properly. The moving human tale needs a different style; the haunting horror another.

Books, whether fiction or non-fiction, require yet other elements of wordcraft and discipline: light and shade, proper balance, believable characters, logical arrangement of ideas and build-up of theme . . .

Since this book is concerned with prose, we won't delve into the equally tricky waters of drama — radio, TV, film, theatre — and all the other disciplines where words are needed. But don't forget you can express yourself in ways other than prose. Your ideas and style of approach might more easily fit the parameters of, say, one-act plays, or TV sit-com, but only you can decide that.

Whichever aspect of writing appeals to you and suits your working methods, you must study its particular needs and techniques. Do this by reading intelligently, learning to be critical. If a story is good, can you say *why* it's good? If you put the book aside after a few pages and never open it again, try to decide *why* it didn't work for you. Similarly with films, radio

stories and so forth. As a reader/viewer/listener you're as quali-
fied as the next person to say what you enjoy; it's only a small
step to figuring out *why* you enjoy it, or not, and therefore
you can also start to see where the writer's talent helped him,
or where she went wrong.

But always bear in mind that tastes vary. Some readers love
and relish light romance; some prefer heavy historicals; others
enjoy humour, or adventure, or crime. In every type of book
or story you read, you'll discover some well-written ones and
some less so. Learn to discriminate between the two. Just
because you don't particularly enjoy a book doesn't mean it's
a bad book, or even that it's badly written, though it might
be. Think about it – analyse, cogitate, teach yourself to be an
objective critic; it will all help your writing.

When you change hats and become the writer, while following the general guidelines for whatever genre you choose, write
something you yourself enjoy. If all else fails – if your work
never illumines a professional typesetter's screen – at least have
fun trying. If you write without enjoyment, simply joining the
latest bandwagon or working to order for the money, it usually
shows.

Finding a market

Having settled on *what* to write, if you hope to find yourself
in print you should next decide exactly which market you're
aiming for. Do this *before* you put pen to paper. *Do not* complete and polish your piece and *then* seek a market for it –
that's like kitting your offspring out with a full school uniform
and then looking for a school that wears those colours.

In the early days, your first 'market' could be one of the
many competitions run by various organizations and groups,
details of which you can find in writers' magazines such as

Writer's News, or sometimes in your local library. Even for these, your work will need to be tailored – written to a certain subject or a certain length. But these competitions are a good way to begin as they do allow a certain latitude in content and style.

Every publisher of books has his own particular list. Every weekly or monthly publication has its individual slant. Some magazines don't take fiction: some will publish work by established authors only: some will give new writers a chance. Some publishers of romantic short stories want only gentle romance; some prefer a mystery element, others a hint of irony, or bleak reality. A short story written especially for *Woman's Weekly* will not fit into *She* without considerable rewriting, nor will it be suitable for BBC Radio 4's short story slot.

I'm assured, by editors and agents who should know, that one of the biggest mistakes made by hopeful writers is submitting material that is either wrong for the market, or has no market. A doctor–nurse romance is stretched to 120,000 words (much too long); or a clogs and shawls saga is written to 70,000 (much too short). Nor is there a market for short stories of 7000 words (too long: *on average* stories should be about 2500 words). You may be able to cite examples which prove this ruling wrong, but they're the exception, often written by experienced writers who have been allowed to break some of the rules; unless you believe yourself to be a literary genius, you shouldn't try to emulate them until you can match their expertise.

For instance, if you want to write a romance for Mills & Boon, you must read romances published by Mills & Boon. Lots of them. Then write something similar. If Mills & Boon don't like it, you will need to rewrite considerably before you try it elsewhere, since this is a very specialized market. Mills & Boon do publish guidelines for hopeful romance writers, as do some magazines that publish short stories. To find out, write to the editor.

Before submitting an article, it's wise to query your chosen editor about whether she would be interested in the piece you're planning. Just give a brief idea of your subject and the way you hope to handle it. She may have a similar article already in mind, or she may ask for a different slant. She may even be so keen she'll ask you to hurry up and finish it, then you can go ahead on a cresting wave of confidence.

You must *read* the magazine you want to write for. Study its content, what length of story or article it takes, what general subjects it prefers; the advertisements it prints will give you a clue as to what reader it's aiming at, and that same readership must be your target. *Don't* send a homely tale about an old lady's love for her little dog to a magazine aimed at pop-mad teenagers. *Don't* ask a railway magazine to publish a piece about stamps. You *must* shape your work to your market.

It would be impossible for me to list the requirements of every publishing house, magazine or journal; tastes change and editors move on, often at an alarming rate. Finding your niche is an aspect of your craft that you must study for yourself if you want to succeed. Read similar books or magazines, listen to the programme: discover what their content is and thus what kind of writing they might buy.

For details of what to do once your manuscript is completed, and how to present it to a publisher, see Chapter Twelve.

Book proposals

Submitting a **non-fiction idea** to a publisher *before* you complete the book is essential. This is called making a book proposal.

To prepare a book proposal, have a clear overview of the form your book will take: work out your framework, then write it down, chapter by chapter, briefly explaining what you plan to do in each section. Complete the first two or three chapters (as an example of your style), and put them with your outline. Preface them with a title page which includes the information that this is a book proposal, and send it off to your chosen publisher with a covering letter *briefly* explaining why you feel your book breaks new ground.

This may seem a lot of work, but it's not so much as finishing the book only to be told there's no market for it. At the very least you will find out if the book is viable. Don't just take the word of one publisher; if the first sends it back then try another, and another. If half a dozen say it won't work, maybe you should rethink. You may be fortunate in being commissioned (i.e. offered an advance and asked to finish the book) solely on the strength of your proposal. Then you can go ahead knowing that someone wants it.

For full-length **fiction**, too, you may prepare a book proposal if you prefer – send the opening chapters (not extracts from the middle) plus a synopsis of the rest (two or three pages may be enough). However, with fiction you're unlikely to be commissioned on this fragment, unless you're an established writer with a proven track record. Receiving a book proposal from an *aspiring* novelist, a publisher may well express interest and ask to see the completed manuscript, but that is no guarantee that he will buy it even when you do finish it.

The drawback to sending book proposals is that you may feel suspended, waiting for a green light to go ahead, unable to either continue that book or turn to something new. In my experience, with fiction you might as well write the whole book and send it off. While it does the rounds, get on with the next, so you've always something new to hope on. Still, the choice is yours. As ever, do it the way that suits *you* best.

Facing the empty page

First, though, as Mrs Beeton never did say, catch your hare. Or, to follow my own analogy, *dig up that diamond*. In other words:

CREATE YOUR RAW MATERIAL

Having done your homework, deciding how, what, and for whom you intend to write, your first goal is to fill the first empty page, then the next, and the next. **Sit down and write**: it doesn't matter how or where.

Give yourself a target – try to do a little each day, even if it's only a page, or a single sentence. Anybody can write one sentence a day and, probably, you'll find that writing it will give you the impetus to go on and write more. Or aim at producing five hundred words a day. It's breaking the ice that counts, getting over that first hurdle.

A ruse that helps you to restart the next day is to stop writing right in the middle of a scene, the middle of a sentence, the middle . . .

I know this trick works, but following it is easier said than done: I will keep going until sentence and scene are all complete and *then* stop, with a sigh of relief, and go and see what my patient husband is doing at whatever hour of the evening or early morning it happens to be. Next day, I may have trouble picking up the reins of a new scene. It's maddening. What I *should* do, if I have to finish one scene before I stop, is write half a sentence of the next segment before I put down my pen or save my file on disk; that would at least give me a hook on which to hang my thread next morning.

But can I remember to leave an end hanging? Not often.

However you do it, try to keep going, day after day with as few days missed as possible, until you finish. The **absolute essential** is to **complete** whatever you're writing, whether it's a rhyming couplet, a letter for the parish magazine, a short story, or a 900-page block-buster novel. Until it's finished, you can't know whether it works or not.

It doesn't matter how rough your first draft is. Once you've captured its essence you can work on it, mould it, transform it, perhaps lengthen it (with caution), and probably cut it (careful pruning *always* improves a piece of writing).

Cutting and polishing your gem

Methods of editing, like methods of working, vary from author to author. Some prefer to create their entire first draft without stopping to re-read any of it. Others have to work page by page, polishing every phrase as they go. Still others start every day by reading over yesterday's work and adjusting obvious faults before carrying on creating the next section.

With the first method, unless you're skilled and careful, you can go wildly astray and need to do massive rewrites; on the other hand, driven by inspiration you might break new ground and expand the frontiers of prose. With the second method, you could work and work on perfecting something that will need altering yet again, or even discarding entirely, when you see how the story works out in the end. The *way* you do it is not important, so long as you choose the method that suits *you*. But I suggest that you resist the temptation to polish too highly until you've completed the piece. You can work and re-work your first few pages and never get any more written.

I have that tendency myself. Thanks for the reminder.

Having done your polishing, there comes a moment when you know your piece is as good as you can make it, for now. Don't expect it to be perfect. Not ever. The day you're entirely satisfied is the day you should stop writing. Your work will seldom, even, be as good as you would dearly like it to be. Maddeningly, the original idea in your mind is always far more sharp and bright than what appears on the page. But that's why we keep writing, trying to capture the elusive butterfly perfection, or at least to draw nearer to it on occasion. For now, you simply make it as good as you can *at the moment*, then send it out to face its public, and turn to your next creation. Don't wait for a reply, start something new. If your first baby keeps returning with nothing but rejection slips, you'll have hopes for your second, and for your third, or your fourth . . .

Even if your first piece never gets published — even if you decide not to send it to any editor — writing it will have taught you something on which you can build for the future.

Trust me. It works.

RECAP

- Find the working method that suits *you* best.
- Decide what to write — what you will *enjoy* writing.
- Choose your market.
- For non-fiction, prepare a book proposal — an outline plan and a synopsis, plus first two or three chapters.
- Sit down and make a start.
- Give yourself a target, a daily quota, however small.
- Complete your first draft.

And, all the time, while reading books, magazines or newspapers, while watching TV or film, while scanning notices or bus time-tables ... cultivate your critical faculty. Think – is this well expressed? Does this arrangement of words convey the meaning efficiently and succinctly? Could it be improved in any way?

Exercise: *Kick-starting your imagination*
This is a good exercise to try if you're really stuck for ideas and want to jerk yourself out of the mire. Using as much free-range imagination as you can, choose and write down nine elements, as follows:

a) **A MOOD:** happy, sad, angry, revengeful, lonely ...

b) **A PROTAGONIST,** or main character: the being who is feeling your chosen mood – man, woman, child; earthling or alien; could even be an animal, or a mechanical object such as a car. Don't play safe – experiment.

c) **A VERB:** decide on a verb of movement. How is your protagonist moving? Walking, running, gliding, sailing, galumphing ...

d) **AN ADVERB** to describe *how* the character is doing whatever he's doing, e.g. walking *slowly*; riding *uncomfortably*; waltzing *energetically* (a word to express your chosen mood would be good). NB As a rule, you should use adverbs sparingly. It's more effective to use a strong verb, i.e. 'she hobbled' is more vivid than 'she moved awkwardly'.

e) **AN ERA:** a time in which to set your piece – past, present or future.

f) **A SETTING:** the place where the story starts. Could be a forest, a town, a distant planet, a beach, a farm, a railway station ... YOU choose.

g) **AN OBJECT**: anything at all — a ball, a firework, a flower
. . .

h) **AN ADJECTIVE** to describe the object — a *red* ball; a
dud firework; a *fading* flower . . . NB Adjectives, too,
should be used with discretion.

i) **NAME** your protagonist.

Finally, use these elements to construct a sentence, beginning
'As . . .'

For example, you might choose fairly safe things like a) a mood
of *happiness*, felt by b) a *woman*, who is c) *walking* d) *slowly*,
in e) *the present day*, through f) *a shopping precinct*, with g)
the object being *a dress* that is h) *white*. Let's call the woman
i) *Ann*.

Your sentence would read: *As Ann walked slowly (strolled?)
through the shopping precinct, the sight of the white dress in
the shop window made her smile with sheer happiness.*

Or you could be more daring and go for a mood of *revenge*,
felt by a *male alien being*, who is *flying erratically*, in *the far
future*, above *a salt desert*, with *a spire* that is *pulsating*. Let's
call this being *Gnert*.

This sentence will become something like: *As Gnert flew
erratically over the salt desert, his vengeful eyes lit on the Spire,
which he could see pulsating in the distance.* (It seemed to me
that the Spire would have even more dramatic impact with a
capital letter. Do you agree?)

This exercise creates a sound beginning — something happening, someone in action, with questions raised in the reader's
mind to make him want to read on. Aren't you curious to
know why the sight of the white dress made Ann feel so happy?
And aren't you longing to know more about Gnert and that

mysterious Spire? By using the nine elements, we've already got the reader hooked. All in one sentence.

Now, choose your own nine elements. The possibilities are limited only by your imagination. Mix and match them as you like. If they're not quite right, alter them to make a more interesting story as you write your sentence. Then, continue writing for five minutes *without stopping*. Write whatever comes into your head, just keep it going. You should find yourself launched into a story which will begin to take shape in your mind and start up other ideas. If this beginning doesn't grab your interest, go back and try again, changing some or all of the elements. Be adventurous. You may surprise yourself.

NB As you read this book, it would be useful if you had some writing of your own to use as a reference example. If you don't already have a piece you can use, try expanding your nine-element beginning into a proper story of publishable length — say, six or seven double-spaced pages.

2 · Back to Basics

Foraging after facts

One of the most important points to consider, before you even begin to write, is whether you need to do any **research**. Never guess at factual information: it's all too easy to make *unintentional* slips without knowingly inventing details. Beware of making assumptions. Accuracy of factual information is *your* responsibility, not something you can leave for your poor overworked copy-editor to sort out.

In my experience, the research should come first, before you begin to develop your story beyond a vague idea. You need the idea, of course, so that you know what subject or era you need to read about. But if you plan too far, you may find that some of your ideas wouldn't work in the context you've chosen, so you'll have to rethink to make it logical. For example, you might need a character to get a message from England to India and you decide he'll make a phone call, only to find that the phone lines weren't connected until ten years later. Happily, useful and unexpected plot twists tend to evolve naturally out of your research. You never know what handy nuggets lie in wait for you.

If you still think you can skimp on research, be warned: every subject, be it the history of your local regiment or current airline schedules, is far more complex than you ever dreamed, with unforeseen traps that might easily catch you out if you don't check your facts. This is not to say that you can't have your intrepid fictional granny fly off to Australia on a wet Wednesday unless you check the airline schedules, but if she flies out *specifically* on Wednesday, 20 July 1994, someone will be waiting to pounce and set you right – that day was a scorcher, and how did Granny get to Heathrow by rail when the trains weren't running because of the strike? If you can equivocate, do so; if you need to specify, get it right. There's always some know-all waiting to write in and gleefully tell you when you trip up.

Good research makes your stories more credible, gives them depth and authenticity, and, as a bonus, widens your education. It can also lead to new friendships and open useful links with experts in various fields. What's more, in unsuspected bywaters you may pan golden nuggets of truth that will vastly enrich your work.

The best place to begin researching is your **local library**. When delving into a subject new to you, try the **children's section** – juvenile books often give a clear outline of the topic, from which you can expand into the adult section. I once tried to get to grips with the French Revolution and failed miserably until I read a book aimed at teenagers. Illuminating! Having grasped the basic facts, I was able to deepen my study without problems. Well-written history can be as easy to read as fiction, especially when you're interested in its subject. But be warned – brilliant historians are not always brilliant writers. They may know their subject intimately, but some of them produce prose like thick, sticky mud – takes hours to wade through and you have to keep stopping to take a breather, review the ground won, and wipe your boots!

Modern technology allows you to search the library's

resources for yourself. Don't be shy of that computer console, the screen gives you all the information you need in order to use the facility. Make a friend of your librarian; involve him in your quest for obscure bits of knowledge. Librarians are trained to do more than stamp books all day; the ones I know seem to relish the opportunity to do some detective work for a change. Maps, old documents, local press clippings . . . You'll be surprised what wealth of information is available for the asking.

In **museums** you can actually *see* the old artefacts, costumes, whatever it is you're after. And you'll find useful books or pamphlets which might have just the information you need. Use them to build up your personal reference library.

An Aladdin's cave of factual treasures waits for you in **newspaper archives**. Searching for one snippet of information can be time-consuming, but the rewards along the way are incalculable; keep your mind open to other possibilities while you're there, you never know what you might stumble across. Among other things, I found a hilarious, satirical 'Letter to the Editor' in our local archives for 1870. I often use it to 'leave 'em laughing' when I go public speaking.

If you can't find your facts already written down, consult the **experts**. Say you want to find out about local council matters . . . DON'T rush up and buttonhole the lord mayor when he's opening a fête, but DO write to your local town hall and tell them your query. A letter is the best opening gambit: the worst your chosen expert can do is ignore it, but he's more likely to write back with the answer, or tell you who else to try, or perhaps even offer to let you come in and search his archives. People are amazingly generous, if you approach them with tact and diplomacy. To give one instance out of many, when I was commissioned to write a novel against a background of the Tulip Parade in Spalding, Lincolnshire, all I knew was that the event took place annually. Via a local newspaper, I discovered the name of the man who organized the carnival and wrote to him asking if he had any brochures or other information available. He responded by inviting me over to his office, where he gave me two whole hours of his time before taking me to meet the men who were making the floats (it's a year-round job) and gave me permission to go back as often as I wished during the months preceding the parade. He also gave me the names of other people who might provide extra information, including a tulip-grower whose daughter had, coincidentally, been chosen as Miss Tulipland one year. That family, too, could not have been more welcoming and helpful. Over a period of time I gleaned ample information to cover all aspects of the run-up to the festival, which made a glamorous, colourful background for the book. We also had the joy of seeing the Tulip Parade for ourselves that year — a sight not to be forgotten. When the book came out, I sent copies of it to all the people who had helped me. Some of them actually appeared in the book, playing themselves. The rest had fun trying to decide exactly which fictional characters were based on them (none were, as it happens).

So . . . don't be diffident: if you're unsure of your facts, then **find out. ASK an expert.** The results might surprise you.

And so, having done your research, you embark upon the actual writing of your tale, at which point you encounter the delights of written English in all its aspects — grammar, syntax, punctuation . . . Here again, if you want to succeed as a writer, you must GET IT RIGHT.

English as she are wrote

During an English lesson at school, when I was thirteen and bored silly with the intricacies of dangling participles, split infinitives, the uses of the pluperfect tense and other esoteric delights whose exact names I have long forgotten, I asked the mistress, Miss Ryder, what was the point of learning all these tedious rules. I have never forgotten her answer:

'You learn the rules,' she said, 'so that you know exactly what you're doing and why you're doing it. Later, when you know the rules inside out, *then* you can break them, with purpose, and to effect.'

That seemed a good answer then and it still seems so now.

If you seriously desire to be published, it's important that you have a firm grasp of written English — the essential tool of your trade. The odd error here and there is excusable and normal — no editor will turn down your work because of the occasional slip — but if you pepper your work with incorrect spellings, bad grammar and sloppy syntax, you are inviting rejection before you have a chance to display your originality, your flair, your sheer brilliance . . .

'It shouldn't matter!' some of you cry. 'Language is only a means of communication.' That's true — but are you sure you use language in a way that conveys your exact meaning to your reader? Remember that the order to 'advance rapidly and try to prevent the enemy from carrying off the guns', sent the Light Brigade charging to destruction because it didn't specify *which* guns it meant.

'English is a living language, changing all the time,' is another old riposte. 'Why should I worry about grammar? Look at this best-selling author who breaks all the rules . . .'

There will always be exceptions. They do not make the basic guidelines any less valid.

For the vast mass of writers – those of us who have neither helpful connections nor beginner's luck, we who are *never* going to find fame by writing pages where expletives, like fat raisins, dot a porridge of ungrammatical regional slang – for us, it's as well to stick to good, plain English (though *plain* is an insult to a language so infinitely rich with meaning and nuance).

Even so, we should know how to manipulate written words to create desired effects, and in order to do so we sometimes need to break the rules of pedantically perfect grammar and syntax. The same can be said of the rules of good storytelling – when you're skilled you can sometimes break the rules, but before you start to experiment you have to know exactly what you're doing. If you break the rules out of ignorance, what you end up with is an amateurish mess.

Judging from my experience with students and group members, many adults have soaked up bad habits from years of writing chatty letters to friends, or perhaps from writing only technical reports and business letters, using stilted, formal words; or from not writing much at all. One lady brought me a story she had written, asking me for a 'critique' – an in-depth analysis. I wrote her a comprehensive reply, pointing out where she might improve her story and adding a tactful note to the effect that her spelling and grammar were, 'as you probably know', somewhat adrift. The lady was furious with me – not for criticizing her English but for assuming that she *knew* it needed correction. 'Of course I didn't know!' she blazed at me. 'I wouldn't have left it like that if I had known, would I? That's just the trouble – when you're an adult, nobody ever *tells* you these things.'

This may be a problem with other writers who begin in later life – they don't notice the bad habits they've acquired, or realize how much they've forgotten from schooldays. For myself, after many years as a student of English, I'm *still* learning, and still noticing, or sometimes failing to notice, mistakes in my own English. If you notice any in this book, write to Father Christmas, North Pole . . .

Younger people could blame the school system for sloppy habits: many of them fell prey to the once-trendy 'you mustn't stifle their creativity by marking bad spelling and grammar' school of thought. One such young man, joining a writing group some years ago, proudly showed me his CSE English language folder, for much of which he had perfect marks, ending with 99 out of 100 as an exam result. I was astonished to find his writing littered with basic errors that had gone unremarked, with the result that his spelling remained chronically awry and his grammar was at times so convoluted as to make his work incomprehensible. By making him think he was a top English scholar, his teachers had done him a sad disservice. What if a future employer asked him to write a letter, or plan a report? Could the boy even have filled out a job application without appearing only half literate?

The problem appears all around us. Look at labels on market stalls, notices outside pubs or in hospitals, leaflets everywhere . . . I amuse myself making a collection of bloopers from such sources. To my dismay, they seem to be proliferating. If *you* have a problem with written language, which you don't feel able to deal with by yourself, don't be too proud to take a refresher course. These are readily available at night schools. Maybe it doesn't matter in some occupations, but if you want to be a writer, a good grasp of English is vital.

This book's purpose is not to teach English, but perhaps it might be helpful if we go over a few of the areas that have emerged as the main sticky patches with my own students and friends.

1. Punctuation of dialogue

Most of us never need to think about presenting dialogue until we suddenly want to write a story; then, the moment a character starts to speak, we have to consider exactly where to put the dots and commas. At school you probably learned to encapsulate dialogue with double inverted commas (now called quotation marks), e.g.: *"Hello," she said.* Today's preference is for single quotation marks: *'Hello,' she said.* Note that the comma goes *inside* the quotes and that the sentence is three words long. You *don't* write it as two sentences: *'Hello.' She said.*

Observant reading can help — see how printed books present dialogue.

Exercise: To test your own punctuating skills, try writing the following with all the correct marks added:
1. You were going to tell me about Bill he reminded her.
2. Do you write under your own name she asked him.
3. He smiled at us both Good morning ladies.
4. Jenny said The children will have to go home early.
5. If we ladies go in for coffee Mrs Fennel suggested the gentlemen can join us later.
6. Did he say poison she asked.

Here's how you should have punctuated the exercise:
1. *'You were going to tell me about Bill,' he reminded her.* The comma goes inside the quotes.
2. *'Do you write under your own name?' she asked him.* The question mark goes inside the quotes. Usually a question mark acts like a full stop, but here *she asked him* is a continuation of the sentence, so *she* keeps a small (lower case) letter.
3. *He smiled at us both. 'Good morning, ladies.'* This is two complete sentences, so a full stop goes after *both*. Also, note the comma before *ladies*.

4. *Jenny said, 'The children will have to go home early.'* This time, the narrative phrase being before the dialogue, the comma comes *outside* the quotes; the speech itself begins with a capital letter, being a sentence within a sentence.

5. *'If we ladies go in for coffee,' Mrs Fennel suggested, 'the gentlemen can join us later.'* The spoken words form a single sentence, so the quotes are broken by two commas, the first inside the quotes, the second before them; the second section of dialogue, continuing the sentence, keeps a small letter at its beginning.

6. *'Did he say "poison"?' she asked.* When putting a quote within a quote, use a different type of quotation marks, as here with doubles inside singles. Also, be careful where you put your stops: in this case, the question mark relates to the whole speech, so it's placed outside the double quotes and inside the closing single.

The six exercise sentences all contain **direct speech** — that is, they repeat the exact words, as spoken. The other method of recounting dialogue is with **reported speech,** which paraphrases what was actually said; this is sometimes useful for brevity, when the actual words aren't important. It often involves a change of tenses. Our six exercise sentences could be **reported** thus:

1. *He reminded her that she had been going to tell him about Bill.*

2. *She asked him if he wrote under his own name.*

3. *He smiled and bade us both good morning.*

4. *Jenny said the children would have to go home early.*

5. *Mrs Fennel suggested that, if the ladies went in for coffee, the gentlemen could join them later.*

6. *She asked if he had used the word 'poison'*. Note that quotes still need to be used for *'poison'*. Note also that, in such cases, the final stop comes *after* the quote mark.

We'll be discussing dialogue and its uses more fully later on.

2. You, me and the gatepost

My husband and I . . . Or should it be *My husband and me* . . . ? Or *My husband and myself* . . . ? Which would you use?

Some people seem to feel that 'I' is always more correct than 'me'; others can't decide, so compound the error by making it 'myself'. The grammatical rule is to use 'I' for the subject of the sentence and 'me' for the object. But, if this kind of technicality turns your brain to jelly, there is a way round it: a simple rule of thumb is to eliminate the other person – the person who goes along with 'I' or 'me'.

E.g.: *Mother gave John and I some tickets for the theatre*. If you take John out of it, it becomes evident that this is wrong: you wouldn't say 'Mother gave I some tickets . . .' So: *Mother gave John and me some tickets*. CORRECT!

Keith and me will be going to London next week. WRONG.

Will you be joining Keith and me? RIGHT.

We all went to London – Keith, John, Alice, Freda and me. WRONG. The first person is included in the 'we', so GRAMMATICALLY it should be *Keith, John, Alice <u>and I</u> (went)*.

However, if you are *purposely* writing in colloquial English, your narrative will include 'common usage' errors of this kind: and, of course, in dialogue you may deliberately let your *character* get it wrong.

Yes, it can get complicated, but, here again, Miss Ryder's words hold good: once you know the rule, you can use it with confidence, and break it, in places, for a specific purpose.

3. Those deadly apostrophes

The misuse of apostrophes is becoming a plague. Many people seem to believe that every time they finish a word with an 's' it has to be preceded by its very own apostrophe: for instance *fish and chip's*, or *fruit scone's* – both of which are wrong. A coffee shop had a trolley for empties, which was marked *FOR TRAY'S* (wrong again), and in a village near us, a chip shop helper had had a rush of ink to the felt-tip and, not content with adding apostrophes to every plural, had made them commas; so the signs advertised *fish and chip,s with pea,s or bean,s*; *fish cake,s and chip,s*; and even *chilled can,s of drink,s*. We wondered if this might be a cunning plan to draw attention, and so we jokingly asked about it. Next time we visited the shop, they were selling grammatical 'fish and chips with peas or beans' . . . Jolly tasty they were, too. With or without punctuation.

In its most common usage, an apostrophe denotes either:
  i) a missing letter or letters.
  ii) a possessive – something belonging to someone/thing.

i) When the apostrophe marks a missing letter, the thing to remember is that **it goes in place of that letter**, e.g. the 'o' left out of the word 'not' in abbreviated verbs such as *wouldn't*; *couldn't*; *won't*; *didn't*: or the 'a' of *we're*; *they're* and so on. If you have a habit of writing could'nt; had'nt; was'nt – spot it and correct it.

ii) When an apostrophe denotes a possessive, it's helpful to think of it as meaning 'of the' or 'belonging to' – e.g.: *The girl's mother* (the mother of the girl); *the boy's handkerchief* (the handkerchief belonging to the boy); *the cowslip's bell*; *a midsummer night's dream*; *tiger's eye*; *tomorrow's dawn*; *a rose's scent* (the scent of one single rose).

The scent of **more than one rose** is written: *the roses' scent*

– in **plurals** the possessive apostrophe comes after the 's'. Hence also: *the Browns' house* (the house belonging to the family named Brown); *the sailors' rum ration* (more than one sailor gets the grog).

You may run into complications, e.g.: *my cousin's dogs' kennel* (the kennel belonging to several dogs owned by one cousin); or, if you want to mention the motor yacht owned by the Jones family, you can write *the Jones' motor yacht* or *the Joneses' motor yacht*. Who do those posey Joneses think they are, anyway? And how do you punctuate it when the car belongs to both Mary and Chris: *Mary and Chris's car*, or is it *Mary's and Chris's car*? Personally, I'd get round it by saying *the Mackies' car*, but what if the couple aren't officially married . . . ?

This being our own wonderful language, there are always exceptions to prove the rule. For instance, when the plural isn't made with an 's', as for *women*, *men* and *children*, the apostrophe behaves as for the singular noun, so you would write *women's magazines*; *men's handkerchiefs*; *children's playground*. Or there's the pronoun *it*, which takes the apostrophe (*it's*) only to signify *it is* or *it has*. For the possessive, as in *the dog wagged its tail*, no apostrophe is used. This applies also to the personal possessives *yours*, *ours*, *hers* – no apostrophe. Thus we write: *'It's been a long time since that washing machine of hers had its last service,' said Fred.*

Similarly, the word 'who': if you write *who's*, it means 'who is' or 'who has': *Who's been sleeping in my bed? Who's that knocking at my door?* The possessive form is *whose* – e.g.: *the man whose house has been burgled*; *the girl whose eyes set his soul on fire*.

This is not a comprehensive essay on the use of apostrophes. For further information, see the list of recommended books on grammar on page 205.

4. Split infinitives

Another source of confusion, 'the infinitive' is the part of a verb that might be called its title – e.g.: to be; to go; to run; to meander; to waffle; to ask; to speculate ... All these are infinitives and, so the rule says, should not be split asunder by putting another word between 'to' and its mate. So rather than writing 'he was told to quickly run to the shop', you would put, *he was told to run quickly to the shop* – 'to run' being the infinitive which should not be split.

Purists argue that this rule is absolute. Others say that at times the effort not to split makes for grammatical ugliness. Fans of *Star Trek* have grown up hearing Captain Kirk of the Star Ship *Enterprise* declare his intention of splitting infinity along with his infinitive with his mission '*to boldly go where no man has gone before*'. 'It wouldn't sound the same if he'd said "to go boldly",' they protest, and I agree – that order of words does weaken the effect. But couldn't he have said, '*Its five-year mission ... boldly to go* ...'? That would have had the same power *and* been grammatically correct.

What do *you* think? Learn the rule and, when you break it, know why.

5. Little things mean a lot

From the discussion of Captain Kirk's 'going boldly', you will see that even the order in which you choose to use words can itself create effects. Try to train your eye, and your mind's inner ear, to become aware of them. Listen to the rhythm. Try reading aloud. Even in prose, words can lilt and sing. Some phrases have great power – *Thine be the glory!* somehow thunders in our minds. Make it *Yours is the glory* and it seems weaker. *The woman fought off her attacker* is a far more striking way of putting it than *The attacker was fought off by the woman*.

Learn to differentiate between sentences and phrases. A

sentence has a finite verb in it and is thus complete in itself; a phrase cannot stand alone, as it has no finite verb. Look again at that last sentence and see how it's punctuated. It's made up of two complete sentences, but since their sense is inextricably linked I've connected them with a semi-colon. The last section *as it has no finite verb* is a phrase, for reasons it states within itself; therefore it takes only a comma before it, to separate it from the main clause.

Stops: another fraught subject, with choices aplenty. An absolute no-no is using commas where you need a longer stop, as in *She decided to wear her shawl, it would be cold at the party.* These are two complete sentences, which need more than a comma between them. If you choose a full stop, be sure the sense warrants such a total halt. A colon is less abrupt but still provides a definite interruption and some people argue that it should be used only to precede a list or explanatory enlargement (see last two sentences of this paragraph). The semi-colon allows an easier flow. It's up to you to choose which is best for *your* purposes in *your* particular piece. In this case, I'd probably choose a semi-colon: *She decided to wear her shawl; it would be cold at the party.* Or turn the second half into a clause: *She decided to wear her shawl, as it would be cold at the party.*

The **dash** is another kind of stop, not quite so bold as using brackets but still an interpolation, generally used for parenthesis – making a kind of aside to your reader. Be sure that you understand its use, that your wording around it is clear and flowing, and be careful not to use too many dashes as they tend to look messy. Ditto **ellipses** (three dots . . .). Unless such devices are essential to your purposes, settle for more conventional punctuation.

Be sparing in your use of **capital letters,** too. They're distracting to the eye and should be employed only when common usage demands them (proper nouns, for instance), except in special cases for special emphasis. I was surprised to discover that ranks such as *prince* and *duke* take the lower case (small letter) except when a name is added: *Prince Charles* or *the Prince of Wales* or *the Duke of Westminster* is correct, but *the prince said . . .* or *when the duke arrived . . .*

Complicated, isn't it?

Even the placing of a single comma can make a world of difference. Consider: *The maid Maisie* and *The maid, Maisie.* The first identifies Maisie as being the maid of that name among several maids; the second tells us there is only one maid in the household and her name is Maisie. Or this: *He looked round,* and *He looked around.* The first implies that he turned his head to look behind him; the second tells us he took his time in scanning his surroundings — all with the addition of a single letter.

Yes, small things can be important: they influence the reader, so you as the writer must be aware of them.

This section has dealt largely with punctuation, which is just one of the basic areas for mistakes in written English. For hints on noting and correcting faults of syntax (correct juxtaposition of words) see relevant segments of Chapter Eleven.

RECAP

Two basic essentials of good writing are:
- Accurate, painstaking research

and
- Clear, correctly written English.

Exercise: Buy, or borrow from the library, a book on English grammar and use it as bed-time reading – you may be surprised how interesting and illuminating it can be. One of my own favourites, which often comes off my bookshelf when I'm in doubt, is *Current English Usage* by Frederick T. Wood, published by Macmillan: clear in its explanations and immensely readable (which is not always the case with reference books – they can be badly written, too). I also recommend the classic *The Complete Plain Words*, by Sir Ernest Gowers, and *Mind the Stop: A Brief Guide to Punctuation*, by G. V. Carey. But there are many others available. Try to get an up-to-date one, too. Even grammar has occasional changes of fashion.

3 · Teach Yourself Criticism
– The World's Worst Story

If you belong to a writers' group or class, you'll know how difficult it is to judge a piece of writing that is being read aloud by its nervous author. A good reader can make a bad piece sound far better than it looks when read silently from the page; conversely, a bad reader can ruin a little gem. Besides which, it's difficult to be direct in your criticism with the author sitting there in front of you – unless you're a sadist who enjoys hurting other people's feelings.

A journalist friend of mine, one-time chairman of a writing group we started in Lincoln, could be cuttingly cruel with beginners: he maintained that if the writer was upset by criticism, went away and never wrote again, that proved he or she wasn't really a writer and the world would never miss his/her output. *Real* writers, he said, might be angry at first, but would use the criticism and come back, either with valid arguments or with a rewritten and improved piece.

He did have a point, but most of us couldn't be that tough on someone whose friendship we might value.

The trouble with writers is, we're over-sensitive – criticizing our work is like saying our darling baby is ugly. Which is why most of us cling to the kind words of family and friends who would rather tell us our baby is beautiful than confess that they've noticed he has elephant's ears. My husband (whose judgement I value) has often been less than flattering about my own work. Adverse comments upset and infuriate me, of course: I am very easily persuaded that I'm no good at writing and should never attempt to do any more. However, having slept on his words, either I can see that he does have a good point or I know why he's wrong and can explain it both to him and to myself. Whichever it is, I believe his input helps me to be a better writer because it lends a different perspective and obliges me to *think* about what I'm doing and perhaps change bad habits I've acquired.

At times, when trying to assess your own writing, you will find that you know it too well to take a fresh, objective view; so an *informed* second opinion is valuable. 'Informed' is the vital word: my husband has learned the techniques of good writing by accompanying me to writers' meetings and conferences over thirty years, and by listening to me bewail frequent problems with my own work. In general, family and friends *do not* make good critics, nor does your local librarian, or little Georgie's English teacher. Such persons won't want to offend you by telling you your work is less than good. Half the time, anyway, they couldn't tell you exactly what's wrong with it, or how to improve it, and that's what you need – not just criticism, but *constructive* comment. Seek it where you can and, when you find it, make use of it.

Warming up your critical muscle

Failing the availability of a critic whom you trust, you can train your own mind and eye to spot flaws. However, expanding your discriminatory powers takes practice. And so, just for fun, here's a chance to stretch that faculty and become both editor and critic.

Imagine you are the fiction editor of a magazine that takes

all kinds of stories from unknown writers (an improbable scenario, but this *is* just a game, after all). A miracle has happened – your mail is light, your desk clear, you have all the time in the world to give to a manuscript which has just slid out of a brown envelope. It's accompanied by the correct return postage and a brief, businesslike letter; it's beautifully printed, thanks to a word processor; the first page shows title, pen-name, number of words and the rights its author, who calls herself Cassandrina Dustworthy, is offering. She has added her real name, and her address, in the bottom corner. She looks as though she knows what she's about.

Let's find out.

As you go, take note of minor flaws – grammar, punctuation, spelling, etc.; then, when you've read it all, consider overall structure. Does it flow coherently and, if not, why not? What do you think of the setting, the characterization, the pace and the shape of the story? Is there anything else which, in your opinion as a reader and a dedicated follower of good writing and good storytelling, could be improved?

Besides noting its faults, can you also say what's *good* about the story?

Blue pencils ready? Have fun! Cassandrina Dustworthy will never know.

THE CHRISTMAS PRESENT

by

Cassandrina Dustworthy

Emily Cartwright was a widow in her late fifties. Emily had grey hair and blue eyes and stood about five foot three inches tall. Emily wore her hair in little curls along her forehead, and her features were sharp, an aquiline nose with high cheekbones and thin lips. But despite her appearance Emily was a kindly, unassuming sort of person, who always kept her home neat and tidy. It was a bungalow, in a non-estate position, in a pretty village in the Cotswolds.

Since her husband had died in tragic circumstances five years ago, Emily had been alone in the world except for her son, James, now eighteen. He had been a lovely little boy, quite and kind, polite and well-manered, he had been his mother's pride and joy. He was good at school, too, always got good reports and the teachers always said what a quite, polite, well-manered boy he always was. And he was an excellent tennis player.

So how, Emily wondered to herself musingly, had it all changed so drastically? The lovely little boy had somehow, over the years, become a difficult teenager who had got completely and utterly out of control and fallen in with a bad lot. Since his father was tragically dead and he got his motorbike it had got even worse.

She had never wanted him to have a motor-bike. She had hated them ever since her brother was so tragically killed during the blackout when he had been a messenger on the staff of the famous Monty. Now, he had been a fine young man, one of the best. It was a tragedy that Fred had been taken so young, Emily sighed to herself. She had always thought young Jim might take after his uncle, but it was not to be, sad to say. He had turned out more like his drunken father.

One day James and his friends met up at there usual meeting place, 'the pub', naturally. There bikes roared into the car park, disturbing those who had gone for a peaceful drink just to quench there thirst on a hot day.

"Well, Jim, what shall we do this evening", enquired big Mick the Irishman? "Sure and there are a couple of Proddies I should very much like to make sorry they were ever born, begorrah".

No, that's boring stuff", replied Jim ironically. "I vote we have a burn-up down the shopping precinct and see what's happening down there. There are a few old laddies we could mug and if not we can smash a shop window or two. It will be super fun''.

Off they went with a very great deal of noise and petrol fumes, causing an innocent motorist to break sharply and almost have a nasty accident.

"What a crowd of terrible yobs", said one of the men sitting in the sunshine at one of the tables outside 'the pub'. "What are the police doing, I should like to know".?

Emily sat watching Coronation Street and wondering what James was doing. He always stayed out so late every night and she never knew where he was, but how could she stop him, he was an adult now. He was eighteen, so the law said, even though to her mind a lad of eighteen was still only a child, even if he was full-grown his emotions were still childish.

Come on, lads'', yelled James loudly as he drove his Cowasaki at high speed down the pedestrian precinct, which was filthy with litter and dog mess, as usual. "Why didn't people ever clean up after themselves?", Emily always said. Jim felt a surge of exhilaration as the powerful machine surged past shops like the wind, sending paper flying and kicking up dust in the faces of the poor people going about there lawful business.

The bikers all laughed and hooted there horns as people jumped out of the way of the really very noisy and dangerous machines.

They came to a particularly well-dressed window of a large emporium. It was brightly lit and had a magnificent display of gifts all wonderfully arranged at various heights on fat pedestals all draped with thick black velvet to set off the colourful goods and tempt the eager shopper into parting with there hard-earned cash. There were lacquered fans of exquisite design, terra-cotta pots with silk flowers arranged in them very tastefully indeed, silk scarves of every hue under the sun, and a dazzling host of other most delightful and attractive goods ideal for Christmas presents for close friends and family. They were all cleverly set out with glittering tinsel and shiny baubles in a masterful display of the window-dresser's art.

James slammed on his brakes and reversed his machine, gazing with greedy eyes at a particularly beautiful brooch. "Mum would like that for Christmas", he thought with an unusual moment of thoughtfulness for the woman who had brought him up and been so good to him and it was time he appreciated all her unselfish love for him down the years. He pictured her by the fire with her knitting, her grey hair and her shawl.

"Oh James", ejaculated pretty Fiona, who he had on his rear seat. "I would so love to have a necklace like that, only Ma hasn't got two halfpennies to rub together since our Dad run off with his fancy woman."

That was enough to goad him into action. He reversed his machine a few yards, so that he was facing the great big window and jammed his foot on the accelerator. The bike leapt forward at great speed and smashed right through the window and landed on its side in the middle of the display amid showers of broken glass and pottery.

Jim leapt off. "Come on lads. Help yourselves!", he shouted with a grin as he snatched up the necklace for Fiona and the brooch for his mother. She was jumping up and down in delight, but looking a bit scared in case the police might come along at just that wrong moment in time.

The others had all climbed in through the hole in the window and were making the most of the unexpected windfall. Eventually, there pockets stuffed with ill-gotten loot, they revved up there machines to a deafening pitch, enough to wake the dead, rousing all the elderly people in a nearby old folks home from there beds with there thoughtlessness. What a racket in the dead of night, enough to give you a heart attack.

As they left, the burglar alarms were jangling ineffectively behind them, to add insult to injury.
Then suddenly a dog ran out. Jim slammed on his brakes but sadly hit him and he was dead before he hit the ground. The motorbike skidded and he felt it getting completely out of control so that he couldn't hold it. It was smashed up against the wall with terrific force. Jim was knocked unconscious and fell to the ground with a terrible pain all through his body.
When Jim came round after several awful days when his poor mother had been driven nearly frantic with worry, he was in bed with a nurse beside him, who told him sadly with tears in her eyes that poor Fiona was tragically dead.
"That's tragic", thought Jim sadly to himself. It will teach me to mend my ways. And it did.
It was the best Christmas present Emily Cartwright ever had.

Comments

Probably nobody ever submitted for publication a story quite so abysmal as 'The Christmas Present', though I've seen one or two that came close to it. However beautifully presented it may have been, a busy editor wouldn't read beyond the first couple of paragraphs.

We can gather what the writer had in mind (more or less) – a 'realization' or 'self-discovery' story, where hooligan James 'comes to realize' the error of his ways. At least, I *think* that's what it was about. If Mrs D. had kept that in mind, she might have written a tighter tale.

As presented here, the story contains an amalgam of basic errors, some of which we all commit in the creative fever of first drafts: spelling and syntax errors; erratic indentation of paragraphs; viewpoint all over the place instead of remaining consistent; author intruding too much; confusion of meaning; characters and situations clichéd; irrelevant facts thrown in . . . The motorbike was a Kawasaki, surely? She's mixed it up with the Ninja Turtles' 'Cowabunga', and how did Jim manage to reverse his machine (twice)? You can't go into reverse on a motorbike.

The list could go on. But Mrs Dustworthy evidently isn't aware of the flaws, or she would never have sent it out like this.

When the MS returns in haste, the author will wail, 'They never even read it! Can't have!' But professional editors don't waste time ploughing through material that's obviously hopeless: this one condemns itself within a few sentences. Did *you* read it to the end, without skipping anything? Or were you riveted to every word, couldn't put it down and found it curiously moving? If so, I should give up writing and stick to reading – you're a wonderful audience.

'The Christmas Present' is riddled with problems. However, for our purposes, it will serve as a useful template for what *not* to do as we continue to explore the mysteries of self-editing.

Exercise: Put yourself in the shoes of a creative writing tutor. Mrs Dustworthy has asked you to write her a critique of this story, giving her advice on how it can be edited and improved. How would you reply?

4 · Building Blocks

Some of the topics in this chapter will be discussed more fully later, but for now let's take an overview of the materials you need to build a good piece of writing.

Any ideas?

If you're really a writer, your head will be full of ideas. The problem is, how to translate them to the page? An acquaintance informed me, rather sadly, that she dreamed up wonderful ideas over the washing-up, but when she came to write them down they never came out as she intended.

'Maddening, isn't it?' said I.

'You mean – it happens to you, too? But I thought it was because I'm not a professional writer!'

Unfortunately, when you try to capture your soaring imagination on paper, you begin to see the flaws in it; the laws of language and logic force you to reshape it; the needs of your market mould it yet again. Your basic idea is like a baby, perfect in the womb but a bit red and wrinkled when it emerges, and in need of some help if it's to become a useful human being. But raising children is one of life's most satisfying tasks: trying to write good prose can be almost as exciting.

*

Your first task is to weigh your baby. Is it a small idea, or a large idea? If it's a cry against dogs that foul your path, then it's probably only big enough to make a letter in the local paper.

Perhaps it's an idea about that old woman down the road, always moaning about the noisy children next door. You visualize a heart-warming story about the way she is transformed when she loses her cat and the noisy children rescue it and bring it safely home – not very original but it may appeal to one of the less trendy women's magazines, especially if you can give it a new twist.

Have you found some new information on the history of a local beauty spot? Then perhaps your idea will make an article.

Or is it a vast, sprawling idea about people caught up in the American Civil War, or events in nineteenth-century Russia? If so, you may be embarking on another *Gone With the Wind*, or *War and Peace*.

The size of the idea will determine the length you need to aim for, and the market you hope to sell to.

Five essentials

To flesh out your idea, you need to gather five Ws: the **who**, the **where**, the **when**, the **why**, and the **what**.

1. The **WHO** means the **characters**, especially the protagonist or main player. He, she, or it, can be either appealing or repellent, but must, above all, be *interesting*. You want your reader to become involved, to care what's going to happen to your player – either want him to be happy, or hope that she gets her just deserts.

2. The **WHERE** is of course the **setting**, the **place** in which the story happens. If it's an everyday location, with which your readers will be familiar (such as a shopping precinct), you need only sketch it in lightly with minimum description. If it's a

strange place – the bottom of the sea, an Amazonian forest, a medieval town, or a distant planet – you must paint pictures with words to let your reader see it as clearly as you do. Remember to draw special attention to *anything that is going to be of relevance* in the story.

3. The **WHEN** is the **time**, which has **three variants**: time of *day or night*; time of *year or season*; and *era* – are we in our own time, or in history, or the future? Or is it a fantasy set somewhen in no time?

4. The **WHY** is the **reason** for the character's being involved. *She* must have some previous history, some motivation for what she's doing as we discover her. *He* existed before he walked into your story. So what now brings them here? No need for detailed explanations at this stage, but that previous life *must be there*, if only in your mind, if these people are to seem real to your reader.

5. The fifth W, **WHAT**, is the **problem** the main character has – if he has no problem he must very soon acquire one, or you have no story, because stories are all about conflict of one kind or another.

Conflict

Although conflict is the driving force of fiction, it doesn't have to be a major confrontation such as a war. There are three basic types:

1) **Protagonist versus nature** – someone crossing a desert, climbing a mountain, exploring the jungle, or simply caught in the rain . . .

2) **Protagonist versus adversary** – a teacher struggling to control her class; a lawman tracking a murderer; villagers fighting to stop a dam, or people complaining about a bad meal . . .

3) **Protagonist versus himself,** fighting some inner demon
   – a man who is terrified of fire must save his family
   from a blaze; a woman knows she is not wise to love
   a particular man, but can't help herself; a child knows
   he shouldn't stray out of the gate, but . . .

A good story will contain *at least one* of these conflicts. A
novel should contain several.

Shape

Before you begin, and while writing, bear in mind the shape
your finished piece needs. Keep a **short story** spare. Concentrate on one theme, one conflict – that's the pivot round which
your plot works: your protagonist is faced with a problem;
how he resolves it provides the story. The piece should build
continually towards its climax, then end with as little delay as
possible. Its shape looks like this:

The peak is the resolution, the culminating moment, the denouement – call it what you will. Everything else climbs towards that
point, every scene, every word relevant to it, and the climax itself
should be succinct – see how the line falls straight down from
the peak. Next time you read a short story, see if it complies with
this basic rule. If it doesn't, yet it still works, ask yourself how
the author has achieved the effect. Could it have been even more
effective if he *had* shaped it better?

In a **full length book,** you have a little more time to linger
– you may stray into a side channel to admire a glorious sunset
along with the characters. But don't linger for too long over

lyrical descriptions; have something happening at the same time. Never forget your pace, never bore the reader or tempt her to skip. Nor must you lose sight of the conflicts. In a novel, many different tensions, minor and major, including examples of all three types explained above, form part of the warp and weft of your plot. Small troubles may be resolved along the way, but others emerge to replace them, and the major thread, which is introduced early on in the book, must not be resolved until the very end.

Books are shaped like this:

Here, the pace rises and falls, ebbs and flows, small climaxes or crises occurring, cliff-hangers to keep your reader page-turning. But still, you will note, it builds all the time, chapter by chapter, towards one final satisfying ending. The winding-up may be a little more lengthy than a short story's, but never let it maunder on for too long.

Style

What *is* style, exactly? It's your unique way of writing, the way you form your sentences and the words you choose to express your thoughts. A close examination of the style of good writers can be illuminating; you might even try imitating them, at first, but if you're to become a good stylist you must develop your own ways with words.

It has been estimated that you need to write a million words before you begin to acquire true style. Remember our first lesson – the only way to learn is to do it. The way to develop a good, individual style is by practice. Write. Write. Write.

Write in a natural way, more or less as you speak, but take more care with grammar and syntax. By all means expand your vocabulary, but keep it unpretentious – remember you're trying to communicate ideas, not show off how clever or how well-read you are. Above all, DO NOT strive for artificial 'literary effect', using embellishments and flowery turns of phrase that do not come naturally to your pen. If you try too hard, it shows and looks absurd. Once upon a time you might have written a business letter saying, *We are grateful for your esteemed communication of the 25th ultimo.* Nowadays, you would put, *Thank you for your letter of 25 May.* Normal, straightforward, everyday words, naturally expressed. Use this basic kind of language and you won't go far wrong. A good tip is to read your work aloud. If anything rings false, sounds clumsy or nonsensical, if it jars in any way, reconsider it.

Plain Anglo-Saxon is the best choice. This writer, she say, '*Elongated sentences composed of excessively polysyllabic words indubitably conspire to produce a manuscript the reading of which resembles a post-prandial saunter through viscous fluidity, serving solely to obfuscate the actuality of one's ultimate intention.*' i.e. **'Long words in long sentences make reading hard work!'**

Viewpoint (VP)

This does not mean the overall stance you intend to take – writing a political thriller about a strike, in which you strongly sympathize with the workers, for instance. Here, **viewpoint** means the eyes and mind of the particular character, or characters, through whom we see the story.

Viewpoint is an enormous subject, with all kinds of variations. For our purposes, we'll look at only the main ones:

1. **Third person, single VP**, which is told entirely from the point of view of one of the characters. This is the most widely used technique in prose-writing.

2. **Third person, multiple VP**, told via more than one character.

3. **First person**, where one of the players is also the narrator − i.e. the author writes *as if he were the character*. Not the same as writing autobiographically, it's more like acting a part.

These three techniques are the most common, but you may also find:

4. **The objective observer** − a narrator who sees all and hears all, but from *outside*; he does not divulge what characters are thinking, only what they do or say. The Bible is written in this style. Its air of lofty detachment does not make for easy reader-identification; I don't recommend it unless your story can't be told in any other way.

Finally we come to:

5. **The omniscient** − a God-like narrator, who sees all, hears all, knows all, including all characters' thoughts and feelings. This VP is difficult to carry off without confusing your reader, but, if you can manage it, good luck!

Since most of us are writing prose that calls for the reader to identify with and therefore care about what happens to the characters, we generally opt for one of the first three VPs on our list. Let's take a closer look at how they're done.

1. Third person, single VP

In this VP, the author describes the drama as if he were an unseen observer, but he makes us privy to the thoughts of **one** of the players. In the following, Elizabeth is the VP character; the author reveals the action, and other actors, through her eyes, coloured by her thoughts and attitudes: *As Elizabeth trailed down the stairs, her hair shining golden in the late sunlight, she wished she did not have to endure the dinner party. With a pang of dismay, she saw her brother Lionel emerge from the drawing room to stand smirking up at her. Oh, God, she groaned inwardly, what was Lionel doing here? He was the last person she wanted to see tonight . . .*

In this piece we 'zoom in' on Elizabeth, observing her approach and seeing the way the light shines on her hair, before going right into her mind. Third person VP allows you the freedom to use distance and/or close-up, as it suits your story, but be aware of which 'camera-angle' you're using and try to move in or out subtly. The word *smirking*, used here, is **her** thought, **her** impression of what she sees, augmented by use of terms like *dismay* and *groaned*; this channels the reader's reaction, too. We have already started to dislike Lionel, haven't we?

Take the same scene, but this time make Lionel the VP character: *As Lionel left the drawing room, his sister Elizabeth trailed down the stairs, her hair shining golden in the late sunlight. She was growing into quite a beauty, he thought, smiling up at her with brotherly affection. 'Liz, my love, I managed to make it after all. Couldn't disappoint my only sister on her birthday . . .'* Here, Lionel is observing his sister's entrance. The fact that her evening is about to be ruined by his arrival will only become clear to him, and to the reader, through her subsequent behaviour towards him. See how our sympathy has switched? He's quite a pleasant chap after all, isn't he?

Thus you play on your reader's susceptibilities, swaying him with your choice of words.

Notice how in these examples the VP character is the first person mentioned – another signal that helps the reader know where he is and with whom he's supposed to identify.

Even if your VP character is the villain of the piece (whom your reader hopes will get her come-uppance in the end), by seeing through her eyes and mind you can show why she acts as she does. We may never like the evil witch, we may abhor what she does, but if you portray her well we shall feel with her and understand what makes her tick.

That's what writing fiction is all about – illuminating aspects of human nature. (And having fun manipulating both characters and readers!)

2. Third person, multiple VP

This variation is useful when you want to show parts of the action that your first VP character doesn't observe, or if you wish to add a different slant to what's happening: you switch to another character's VP (or more than one) from time to time. However, the transition has to be done carefully and you must make the change clear to the reader. Usually, you stick to one VP inside a scene, or perhaps for whole chapters at a time – you don't chop and change *within scenes*. It *can* be done, but it takes some skill to avoid confusing the reader.

For our purposes, we'll assume you're going to take one VP for one section of narrative, then switch to a new one for the next bit.

On the page, such shifts are generally signalled by a break – the end of a chapter, or perhaps simply a double space between paragraphs. So we continue our story, using Elizabeth's VP, accompanying her through a tense family dinner party, until:

At last, Elizabeth was able to make her escape. Thank heaven that was over, she thought as she wearily climbed the stairs. What a total bore Lionel had become. What a disaster this entire evening had been!

Clouds drifted across the moon as Lionel strolled out to the terrace, lighting a cigarette. Drawing smoke deep into his lungs, he stared across the shadowed gardens, wondering what on earth had been wrong with Liz tonight. She hadn't been herself at all, hadn't laughed at his jokes, hadn't even bothered to rise when he teased her . . .

The break in print makes it clear to the reader that there is to be a transition, in this case a switch of VP from Elizabeth to Lionel. Such breaks can also signal a change of scene, or a gap in time. Do it clearly, then your reader will know where he is and the transition will be smooth – he won't even know it's happened.

But he *will* notice if you do it *badly*: *Lionel left the drawing room to see his sister Elizabeth coming slowly down the stairs. Oh God, what was Lionel doing here? Elizabeth had been wishing she could avoid the evening's jollifications but there stood Lionel, smirking. How surprised she would be to see him, he thought. 'Hello, Liz. Happy birthday . . .'* Do this and your reader will feel like a spectator at a tennis match, swapping from one to the other, never knowing where he's supposed to be – ping-pong point-of-view, in fact. Avoid it.

3. First person VP
In the first person viewpoint, the author actually 'becomes' one of the characters: *As I trailed down the stairs, wishing the evening over, Lionel emerged from the drawing room and stood smirking up at me. Oh, God, what was he doing here? He was the last person I wanted to see tonight.*

What you *can't* do with this 'I' VP is to tell us what Lionel is thinking, except through Elizabeth's perceptions: *He looked pleased to see me*. Nor should you include that phrase about her hair. If you write, *I trailed down the stairs, my hair shining in the light* ... the woman sounds incredibly vain and self-obsessed. Or maybe you wanted her to seem that way ... ?

While using first person VP, you have a few extra hurdles to leap. Take care never to step out of character: avoid saying, *My eyes scanned the scene* ... Say, *I gazed at the scene* ... or, even better, just describe what 'you' are seeing: *The valley lay desolate under a bitter sky* ... Never stand back and **observe** the narrator; always write as if you're *inside* her or him. Next problem is how to recount a scene at which your 'I' is not present. You can't have other characters constantly sending vital letters, or rushing to relay important bits of the plot, nor can the narrator eavesdrop too frequently. Make sure that she is the **pivotal** character of your story, so that she's on stage and up to her neck in the action most of the time. Also, assuming her looks have some bearing on the plot, find tricks of describing her in a way that sounds natural. Having her sit in front of a mirror and describe her own reflection has become a cliché. Consider not describing her at all; let your readers imagine her as they wish. As a regular listener to BBC Radio's 'The Archers', I don't recall any of the characters ever being 'described', as such. One of the other characters might say, 'You're going a bit thin on top,' or, 'You look wonderful in that ...' or, 'That new vicar's a bit of a dandy, isn't he?' Given such small clues, I've built up my own idea of what each of them looks like. (Sadly, few of my mental pictures resemble the actors who take the parts; so their public appearances tend to shatter my illusions and I wish they'd remain anonymous behind their microphones!)

One author sweepingly dismissed the use of the first person narrator as 'a beginner's mistake'. Perhaps she meant that beginners tend to write as themselves when they try that VP.

Given the right kind of story, the first person is as effective as the third person, and can have advantages. Many of the best stories have been told in this VP. I've found it especially effective for mysteries, where the main character's misinterpretation of clues can be used to mislead the reader. You leave hints of the truth between the lines, so that the reader suspects when the narrator's reasoning is wrong but is left to figure out the whys and wherefores for himself. This allows the author to heighten tension and keep pages turning until the unsuspecting narrator walks right into the traps laid for her and . . .

Trouble is, you never can tell if your own work is effective; you just do your best and hope. All I can say is that my publisher kept buying my romantic mysteries, the stories sold in umpteen languages, they're borrowed by the thousand from libraries and I keep getting offers for yet another edition to be published somewhere in the world. So they can't have been too bad.

Close-up, head and shoulders, or full-length portrait?

Knowing how much, or how little, of a character's thoughts to reveal is another skill a writer must develop. Is this a deeply introspective story, where much of the plot is concerned with the hero's striving to understand himself and others? If so, linger in his thoughts frequently. Or is it a more external story, where action is more important than psychology?

As a clear example of an action story, think of a western. In this type of book your reader wants to know what's happening, who's saying what, which ranch or canyon they're heading for and who they're shooting at. He isn't so interested in the sheriff's agonizings over the ethics of whether to shoot first or risk his life to give the baddie a chance at a fair trial. Which is not to say you couldn't write a psychological western with a deep-thinking, introspective hero, but be aware that you risk straddling two genres and satisfying readers of neither. Of course, if you can do it brilliantly, there's always room for a great book that breaks new ground.

Watch out for different uses of **viewpoint**, good and not so good, in the examples we'll be studying throughout this book.

Author's voice

Next out of our box of building blocks is stylistic tone of voice, which simply means the literary attitude you strike – the mood you create. Will it be humour, pathos, eroticism, horror? It's all to do with the words you choose and the turn of phrase you employ – flippant, introspective, blunt, slangy, dramatic, chatty, literary, quirky, fantastical . . . ? Think of the style of Mickey Spillane's thrillers; the voice adopted by Conan Doyle as Dr Watson; the light-hearted quality of Jilly Cooper's fiction. All so different from each other, but equally effective.

Whatever you decide, the style has to be suitable to its subject and to the VP character, subtly echoing his attitude to what's happening. If you're using a lot of his thoughts, then you should also use his way of shaping those thoughts, choosing vocabulary that he would use and making analogies appropriate to his experience.

For example, this first person narrator is a puppy in a pet shop, on Christmas Eve. He and his sister Elsie – the ugly one of the family, in his opinion – are the only two pups left in the pen and their dinner is late because the owner of the shop has been busy. So the pup is hungry and irritable. Yet another customer has arrived, with two boys who have been in before:

Here comes Grubby Hands: grrrh.
'Boys, take your hands away, you've frightened him.'

Me, frightened? She's even sillier than I thought. Now he's picked up Elsie. Wait till they see her face!

'Oh, isn't she adorable?'

How can she say that? She should get some of those things people balance across their noses.

Coloured bits of paper being handed over. Maybe now I'll get my dinner.

He doesn't realize that his sister has been bought, leaving him alone . . . The story has pathos (all humour needs a touch of pathos) but it's amusing, too, because of the pup's perceptions. He's very young and hasn't yet learned the word for spectacles, or money, so he describes them in words he does know. On the other hand, if he doesn't know the word for spectacles, would he understand that they improve vision? Does it matter? Hardly fair to ask you to judge on a fragment taken out of context, but all such things have to be weighed and considered if your story is to work. (Find out how this story ends in Chapter Ten.)

Here's a piece of close-up third person VP:

Jess never forgot lounging there in luxury, being waited on and given food like she'd never had before. First came the arrowroot, which tasted strange – 'It's flavoured with sherry wine,' Miss Peartree said as she spooned the mixture from a tumbler. Sherry wine! Jess thought in amazement; she wasn't sure she liked the taste. And then there was the soft-boiled egg and the thin bread and butter. Lord, this was a dream, but she was determined to enjoy it while it lasted. Sooner or later the questions would start, and then she'd be out on her ear, if not carted off to jail in chains, on her way to the gallows. But for now . . . for now it was wondersome.

In this extract the tone is one of awe and uncertainty: we are in Jess's VP, sympathizing with her and learning more about her from her attitude to the food she's given. *Like she'd never had*, while not correct English, is her way of putting it. Similarly *out on her ear* and *carted off in chains*, while being clichés, are in character here because Jess thinks in clichés. The word *gallows* is appropriate because this is a historical novel and the word *wondersome* is pure Jess. In other parts of the book, where the viewpoint steps back a little to be more objective, the style also alters, to more formal English. Use your judgement in order to add this light and shade.

A short story begins in a completely different tone: '*Christmas! You can keep it! Sylvia, just look at those two slobs. Done nothing but booze and eat, eat and booze, all day. And talk! Golf, golf, golf . . . Let's you and me go in the den and maybe I'll tell about my Christmas when . . . well, we'll see. Bring the gin . . .*' Here, we have a comical tale told in the speaker's own slangy style, talking woman-talk to her best friend and promising some amusing confidences.

A non-fiction example: *The worst bone of contention was the flooring: experts insisted that, since it had once been a stable, the only possible authentic material was extremely expensive York stone. The manageress argued that, since it was now to be a restaurant, she would prefer something more level and less likely to accumulate dirt. The experts, however, had their way. In consequence, the restaurant floor is nigh impossible to keep clean, and the wobbling tables have to be adjusted by sticking bits of card under their legs. 'Nuff said.* This is written in a chatty, colloquial style to suit the light-hearted book of which it's a part. But note that it, too, strikes an attitude – it comes down on the side of the manageress, against the experts. So, it's manipulating the reader's sympathies just as the fiction extract did.

Literary tone of voice can make or mar your work. If your style is dull and repetitive, your piece will not come to life, however interesting the subject matter may be. One writer may pen a witty, scintillating piece about a trip to the supermarket: another person can turn an article on a Barbadian holiday into a bore. If you doubt me, think of the letters you receive from friends — some of them are fascinating; others commonplace and pedestrian. All because of the writer's style.

Baiting your hook

All the time, in order to keep your reader hooked, your narrative should include little hints and telegraphs of what is to come. Make the reader desperate to know what's going to happen; tantalize and titillate him by raising questions without immediate answers. But do it subtly. *Little did Jarvis know that in two days' time he was going to meet his murderer* . . . is too obvious. Try something like, *Jarvis jerked round; the street was empty, but still the hairs on his nape stood up tingling. Why did he have the feeling he was being followed?* (Why, indeed? Now you've got your reader wondering, too.)

'Oh, I shall never marry.' Despite her smile, the bleakness in her eyes said she was not joking. (What's wrong with *this* lady, then?)

Did you notice the narrative hooks in the VP samples earlier? Elizabeth *wished she did not have to endure the dinner party. With a pang of dismay, she saw her brother Lionel emerge . . . He was the last person she wanted to see tonight . . .* All of which invites the question: Why? Your reader will read on to find out.

Look again at the extract with Jess as heroine: *Sooner or later the questions would start, and then she'd be out on her ear, if not carted off to jail in chains, on her way to the gallows.* (What secret is this young woman hiding?)

Keep on doing this, in various ways, and you'll produce unputdownable fiction!

Use details for authenticity and atmosphere

You will need different details for different styles of work. In a thriller, real locations, make of car and small touches like brand of cigarettes help realism; in a crime story you may need to explain police procedure, how poisons work, what it feels like to be shot; stories of human interest need *feelings* to the fore; in a romance, describe everything sensually.

YOU decide what details are necessary for your particular piece: maybe all of the above and more; maybe some in one scene, different in another. But please make them *authentic and accurate*. It's vital to get not only your main, important facts right, but minor, apparently trivial detail, too. Check and check again. If it can be verified, verify it.

On the subject of detail, don't accept those taken-for-granted truisms as being inevitably correct. Not all buds are green in the spring: Shakespeare's observation on the subject '*black as ash buds in the front of March*' made me look again and, sure enough, when they first begin to show, the buds of ash trees *are* black. Ruth Rendell observed that the first flush of early spring is more red than green: take a look at willows in February, when their sap is rising – their slender branches are an amazing orange. So, don't rely on other people's observation, look for yourself, use your own perceptions, especially if you can add an original slant to an old theme and make your reader take a fresh look at the world.

Remember, though, that the more detail you use the more you build up importance, so make sure whatever you're describing warrants the emphasis you have given it.

Theme

Whatever you're writing, fiction or non-fiction, short story or book-length, it will be better structured if you clearly decide on its **theme**. This has to do with what motivates your protagonist: loneliness, revenge, desire, self-discovery, the need to find a place, to reach safety . . . A theme can usually be expressed in a single phrase.

An article's theme might be simply 'The sheer terror/delight/tedium of that trip through the Andes' (three variations in **mood** to choose from). A story concerns how 'John decides that he has only himself to rely on', or 'Loneliness of rich old woman eased by kindness of homeless urchin' (a real tear-jerker, that one!). A novel could have as its main thread 'A woman's search for her roots'. And a non-fiction book might be 'Amusing experiences of a bus conductor', or even 'Helping writers to edit their own work'.

Think of books you know and try to decide what theme they have. For example: *Wuthering Heights* = unrequited passion leads to misery; *Pride and Prejudice* = clash of personalities, one proud, one prejudiced; *Gone With the Wind* = Scarlett's feisty but wilful nature proves both her salvation and her undoing.

If you have your theme at the back of your mind as you write, it will keep you on the right track, like a guiding star in the desert.

Motif

While not essential, a motif can be used like a string on which you thread the beads of your plot. It doesn't have to be of enormous significance (though it can be); it's just there to help hold the thing together, to unify and round off your story. It can be a tree which your characters see changing with the seasons; an item of clothing (the red underpants the murderer always wears when he goes out to kill); a piece of music heard now and then, a line of poetry, a shared memory ... Motif can also provide your title: *The Ivy Tree*; *The Robe*; *The Pink Panther* (which was a jewel, if you remember). The best motifs spring from the story rather than being planted artificially.

Other equipment

Other things you will need in your quest to become a better writer include: well-honed powers of description; a smattering of psychology, in order to understand and portray even the most unsympathetic of characters; an ability to write action scenes; an ear for realistic dialogue; an eye for light and shade; a sense of rhythm ...

Still with me?

Examining our example

Was our story 'The Christmas Present' well constructed out of these basic elements? Let's take it point by point.

Mrs Dustworthy's **idea** was for a story about a wild teenager who came to his senses. Her **who** is Emily and her son; her **where** is somewhere in England (the characters live in *a village in the Cotswolds* and the action, we assume, takes place in a nearby town), which for this story is sufficient; her **why** is Jim's wilful search for excitement; and the **what** is the trouble he gets himself into. **Conflicts** include Emily's worry; misunderstandings between her and Jim; the bikers versus the townsfolk; the damage to the window; and the fatal accident to poor Fiona. So far, so fairish.

But her **when** lets her down: we assume the time is contemporary; but Jim thinks of his mother *sitting by the fire with her knitting, her grey hair and her shawl* (she's in her fifties!). We're not told the time of year, or the time of day, until one third of the way through the tale, when a *hot day* is mentioned, with the men at the pub *sitting in the sunshine*; or is it *evening*, as big Mick says? Emily's watching *Coronation Street*, but in town people are *going about there lawful business*; at the same time, the shop window is *brightly lit* and full of Christmas presents, tinsel and baubles . . . Maybe we're in Australia! After the robbery, we're informed that it's *the dead of night*. Doesn't know *when* she is, does she?

Viewpoint is equally confused, a trap many beginners fall into. In a story so short, it's best to use one VP *only*. Here, we start out as an *objective observer*, describing Emily from a distance. We then take Emily's VP, inside her thoughts. Next we're the o.o. again, watching the scene with Jim and friends at the pub; back to Emily; back to Jim (with the author poking her nose in to give us her opinion about litter). Through whose eyes are we supposed to be seeing that minutely described shop window? Makes one wonder if Mrs D.'s a frustrated window-dresser, doesn't it? Next we cut back to Jim, right into his head with his thoughts – but are they *his* thoughts? That *unusual moment of thoughtfulness* is not in character for the yob we've come to know and love, is it? Back to the o.o. for the smash and grab, with the disapproving Mrs D. never far away; then back to Jim (though how did he feel that *terrible pain all through his body* when he was already *knocked unconscious*?). Finally o.o., then Jim, then Emily . . . Or is it? I'm lost.

Learn to watch for these jumps. If you have good reason to make them, then do it with skill and with purpose. Mrs D. commits her errors blatantly, because she doesn't know better. And what a pig's ear it makes of her story!

The **tone of voice** I would categorize as curmudgeonly, disapproving, carping . . . The author, not the VP character, reveals all her personal prejudices. The **shape** is ragged: the story does have a high point, of sorts, but she doesn't reach it very gracefully. Her **theme** is 'a sinner brought to repentance'; and her **motif**, if there is one, could be the motorbike, which Emily hates but which is Jim's joy and also the means of his come-uppance.

Did you manage to write a critique for Mrs D.? If she had been a pupil of mine, I would probably have suggested she use what she's learned from writing this one to help her do better next time. Between ourselves, I fear 'The Christmas Present' is terminally uneditable, with mistakes in every sentence. Mrs Dustworthy might do well to take up macramé instead.

RECAP

Starting from an initial **idea**, build on it, using:
- **The five Ws** – who, where, when, why and what – character, place, time, motivation, conflict.
- **Shape** your story with **viewpoint, tone of voice, theme** and **motif**.
- **Hook** your reader with hints and telegraphs.

Exercise: Using a piece of published writing that you've already read and enjoyed, examine it with these building blocks in mind. See how the writer has carried out his blueprint. Does it work well? Or is the edifice a bit shaky? Even a published story by a great writer may have hairline cracks. Teach yourself to spot them and learn from them.

Continue to examine your own work in the same way.

5 · Story Openings

It has been said that the ideal plot should contain four things: religion, the aristocracy, sex, and crime. Some wag suggested that the perfect opening, therefore, might be: *'My God,' said the Duchess. 'I'm pregnant. Who dunnit?'*

But in the real world . . .

If you did the exercise at the end of Chapter One, taking nine elements as building blocks, you should have at least the beginnings of a story to work with. If not, don't worry – we have 'The Christmas Present' as a template, and we'll be looking at several other examples, both good and not so good. They will give you some idea of how to go about self-editing, by applying the same critical criteria to your own work.

In my researches for this book, I asked editors and agents of my acquaintance for their own tips and pet hates: what is it about a manuscript that appeals to them or appals them? One of the things they all said was that the **beginning** of a piece – book, story or article – is vital: it must be immediately interesting, from page one, ideally from the first sentence. If you haven't grabbed attention by page three, your editor may not read on. One did say that if she's feeling especially well-disposed she may continue to page fifty of a book, but if it hasn't totally engaged her attention by then she'll find something more interesting to do, like scrubbing the floor.

Don't worry too much about writing an irresistible opening in your first draft; you may need to get well established in your story and characters before you can even see what the ideal beginning should be. But if you bear the need for an immediate hook in mind, it will make your life easier.

Peering closer into openings

To interest and involve your reader as soon as possible, a good ploy is to **reveal your main character at or near a point of change**, a crossroads in life, a moment when everything has gone wrong and her world is upturned. Plunge straight in with action and/or dialogue. But don't make your opening so frantically, vividly, shatteringly exciting that what follows falls flat. If your character is struggling with a rapist in the first scene, what further horror can you dredge up for later? Or is she just the first victim — is the rapist your leading actor? Ah, well, then you've started a whole other sort of story.

The choice is yours — the writer's — but since your story must always build up to its ending, it's easier to begin more quietly and work up to the climax.

Check that your first few paragraphs include the five Ws discussed earlier: who, where, when, why, what. At this stage, don't add too much detail; say just enough to whet the reader's appetite and orientate him in the right direction. In some stories it will suit your fictional purposes to keep certain details unclear for a while. It's a question of balance: you need to tell enough to rouse interest while leaving many things unexplained, to keep the reader asking questions, turning pages in the hope of finding out. You slowly unravel the mystery as the story develops, raising more questions in the process, baiting *narrative hooks* to draw the reader along right to the end, when you reveal the solution to the final problem or draw back the seventh veil . . .

Given the kick-start exercise, which ended Chapter One, one of my students chose as his elements:

a) A mood of *anger*, felt by b) *a dwarf*, who was c) *shuffling* d) *angrily*. The era e) was *some time* (this being a fantasy), set in f) *a cave*, with g) the object being *a stone* that was h) *black*. The dwarf's name i) was *Molog*.

The student began a sentence with *As* . . . and, given five minutes to carry on writing, came up with:

As Molog the dwarf shuffled angrily through the cave, he jabbed his foot on a black stone. The sole of his boot grinned open and Molog fell splat on his face.

'Ruddy cobblers!' His bass mutter stirred the echoes in the cavern as he sat vainly trying to make the leather sole stick back into place. His errand was urgent, his journey a long one barely begun. When he got back he'd have something to say to that boot-mender who'd relieved him of half a gold piece only yesterday.

Muttering curses on all cobblers, and white knights, and half-baked imbeciles who fancied themselves royalty, he picked up the stone that had caused his downfall and was about to hurl it into the vasty black deeps of the cave when he noticed something strange about it.

This is excellent. It begins with the character in action and he turns out to be an engaging if bad-tempered chap, in whose fate we immediately become interested. The five Ws are all in place and with three brief paragraphs a fantasy fan will be hooked, already intrigued and asking questions: Who is Molog? What urgent errand is carrying him on a long journey? Why is he in such a foul mood? And what's this about white knights and imbecile royalty? Such insubordination from a dwarf is interesting, and promises plenty of conflict to come. Lastly, what is 'strange' about the stone? We can't wait to turn the page and find out . . .

When you use the kick-start exercise you can't help but write a good opening (nearly) every time. But of course such a beginning may not suit your style or your subject. Nevertheless, however you choose to start, the five Ws should be there somewhere, near the beginning, and so should the narrative hooks.

Did Cassandrina Dustworthy 'get it right' in any way? Let's take a closer look at *her* first three paragraphs:

Emily Cartwright was a widow in her late fifties. Emily had grey hair and blue eyes and stood about five foot three inches tall. Emily wore her hair in little curls along her forehead, and her features were sharp, an aquiline nose with high cheekbones and thin lips. But despite her appearance Emily was a kindly, unassuming sort of person, who always kept her home neat and tidy. It was a bungalow, in a non-estate position, in a pretty village in the Cotswolds.

Since her husband had died in tragic circumstances five years ago, Emily had been alone in the world except for her son, James, now eighteen. He had been a lovely little boy, quite and kind, polite and well-manered, he had been his mother's pride and joy. He was good at school, too, always got good reports and the teachers always said what a quite, polite, well-manered boy he always was. And he was an excellent tennis player.

So how, Emily wondered to herself musingly, had it all changed so drastically?

This is turgid stuff. And, having read the rest of the story, we know that most of it is irrelevant: it's not important for us to know what Emily looks like, or where she lives. Certainly not in such minute detail.

To begin with, the text is riddled with clichés: *neat and tidy*

. . . in a non-estate position . . . in tragic circumstances . . . alone in the world . . . his mother's pride and joy . . . changed so drastically . . . phrases you hear everywhere, all the time, words so over-used they seem welded together. Yes, they do slip in naturally, without your noticing, but you should watch for them and weed them out when you edit, finding some more original way of expressing the same thought – always assuming the thought is *relevant*.

That question should be in your mind the whole time: **Is it relevant?** Does it add anything to the plot, the meaning, the emotion, to character development or to atmosphere? If not, discard it. Much of what Mrs D. has told us has no bearing at all on what follows. If she cuts out the weeds she will see the lie of the ground better, and have space for improvement.

Other blatant faults are the repeated mis-spellings of *quiet* and *well-mannered*. Do this once and it could be an excusable typing error; do it more than once and it tells an editor you're a bad speller who doesn't check. It's no sin to be a bad speller – many of us are – but you should know if you have this tendency and keep a check on yourself. There are plenty of spelling aids around.

By the way, be wary of relying too heavily on your word processor's spell-check device; it will not pick up mistakes like *quite* instead of *quiet*, since it recognizes both of these as proper words – it cannot relate them to context. Throughout 'The Christmas Present', Mrs Dustworthy also constantly mis-spelled *their* – she kept putting *there* (did you notice?) – another fault her spell-check mechanism didn't spot. That's the trouble with computers – they're such logical, literal beasts!

Unnecessary repetition of the name Emily is an added irritant. After introducing the character by name, a simple 'she' would have done. Why must we constantly be reminded that the only character on-stage is called Emily? Who else would we imagine the author was telling us about?

A kindly editor will excuse the odd human error of this kind, but if you pepper your story with petty annoyances even the most generous reader will lose patience.

The second paragraph is equally bad. We already know the character is a widow; the *tragic circumstances* of her husband's death are (apart from being phrased in cliché) so vague as to be meaningless, and anyway it's not important to the story. The repetition of *quiet, polite and well-mannered*, even if properly spelled, could have been avoided. In the third sentence, Mrs D. uses the word *always* three times; she should have noticed that and cut out two instances. Try to avoid using the same word more than once in a short space.

And why has the author thrown in the information that James was an excellent tennis player? Perhaps she thought she was rounding out his character by giving him a sporting skill. Instead, it's yet another irrelevance. Now, if the plot had contained a scene where the boy was required to throw something, really hard, *then* it might have mattered that he had a strong right arm because of wielding that tennis racket; but, as Mrs D. hasn't used the detail to add anything to the story, she should have cut that out, too.

The final sentence does bring us, at last, to the point: the change in James. But it's badly expressed: *So how, Emily wondered to herself musingly, had it all changed so drastically?* If a person 'wonders' she naturally does it to herself and generally 'musing' and 'wondering' are synonymous, so *Emily wondered* is enough, and cut the rest, possibly including *so drastically*, which adds nothing to the sense — remember, take care in using adverbs unless they're vital. Be economical with words at all times, but especially in a short story, where every word should add something to the whole.

What we have so far could have been edited down to: *James had been a lovely little boy, quiet and kind, polite and well-mannered. So how, Emily wondered, had he turned into such a difficult teenager?* Two short sentences succinctly express what the author is trying to convey at this point. They also provide a narrative hook, making the reader wonder, with Emily, how the change has happened. The rest of the story should include the explanation, and find a resolution to Emily's problem.

Examples

Having looked at two examples of openings – one obviously good and one blatantly bad – I'd like you to consider some more examples, and have a go at editing them if only mentally.

I don't usually tell my students exactly *how* to rewrite: I prefer to make suggestions that they are free to take up in their own way, or not take up at all. After all, since they are the writers their final judgement is what matters – how *they* choose to write their piece. Below, though, I have added, to some of the examples, ideas of how rewriting could be achieved. Study them closely, and feel free to disagree if you wish. The whole purpose of this book is to help you to learn to judge for yourself.

―――――― o ――――――

The thin layer of snow marked the straight furrows of the perfectly ploughed fields, accentuating the slight rises in what had appeared to be a completely flat surface. In the autumn I had watched the tractor drivers at work and admired their skill, but today a panorama of art work was before me. The Fenland fields stretched to the distant horizon with only an occasional row of bare trees to break the continuity. The only building in sight was an old derelict cottage nearly a mile away. A week after moving into Filldyke House we had walked across to the cottage to meet our nearest neighbours only to discover as we approached that it was empty. Obviously it had not been lived in for a number of years; windows were boarded up and a heavy padlock was on the door. It had turned out that the nearest occupied house was nearly two miles away in the opposite direction. We had seen children in the garden but had not met the family. Technically we were in the parish of Walton Fen but only went into the village about once a week. The parish priest had visited when we first arrived and we had registered with the local GP. What we didn't know about Walton was soon put right by Mr Collison the village shopkeeper, a rather rotund jolly man, who appeared to know everything about everybody. Unlike many small communities Walton still had a sub post-office and its own primary school, the older children having to travel by bus to the town of Walton Market about nine miles to the west. There was a rather large church for the size of the village and a much smaller Primitive Methodist Chapel nearby . . .

Comments: In this first exploratory draft the writer is doing her thinking on the page, working out the background instead of getting on with the story. If this is the way you work, that's fine, but remember to revise and cut out all the dross. Details about the school, the priest, the doctor, unless they have some bearing on the story, can be 'taken as read' – they're only interesting if they *differ* from normal practice. So, in fact, much of this paragraph can be left out. It is, anyway, over-long by modern standards (it's sad but true that many readers today will skip long passages with no breaks).

The writer should also be careful with those adverbs and adjectives: some of them need pruning. But then, this is a very rough draft; it needs a lot of work before it's ready to be assessed.

———— o ————

The harvest moon shone over the quiet suburb. To its shining eye, all looked peaceful in the empty streets. The houses were shrouded in darkness – not a light gleamed anywhere. No footfalls echoed on the pavements. A bicycle whispered through the dead streets, ridden by a man with a grey, weary face. The ululating wail of a siren shattered the night. One could almost feel the tremor that ran along the row of houses, as the warning blared. The occupants knew they faced another wakeful night of fear.

Comments: This author might consider whether her tone of voice – her prose style – is appropriate to the mood she's trying to convey. To my inner ear, this piece falls flat. Every sentence is a statement, with little variation, the main clause coming first; and length of sentences is too similar. It falls into a rhythm that will quickly become monotonous.

At times, you may *want* to affect your reader with a repetitive pattern – short, choppy sentences can add tension; longer ones can combine to make descriptive, restful passages. But I don't feel that this author has considered the effect her style has on her content. Trying to create the feeling of a quiet, peaceful night, she should have used longer, flowing sentences to set up a restful rhythm; then she could have shocked us with a brief, stark statement about the intrusion of the siren.

Short words add tension, too. In this case, the word *ululating*, while not being wrong, detracts from the tension rather than adds to it. Remember what we've said before about pruning adjectives. In this case, the strong noun *wail* is enough: *The wail of a siren shattered the night.*

Viewpoint is a little shaky – the writer hasn't properly decided what VP she's using. At first, we see through the moon's eye, then we're told *One could also feel* ... Which one? Who is the 'one'? Then we're with the occupants as they *faced another wakeful night* ... Three changes of viewpoint in so short a space is too many. It might be edited thus:

The harvest moon shone over the city, lighting peaceful streets where houses lay shrouded in darkness and no footfall echoed along shadowed pavements. Only the whisper of a bicycle disturbed the stillness, ridden by a man with a grey, weary face, yawning as he made for the comfort of his bed.

The wail of a siren split the night. A tremor seemed to run along the street. The occupants of the houses jerked awake, to face another night of fear.

In this version, our **viewpoint** remains that of an outside observer. Note how the first paragraph is written in leisured sentences, while the second adopts a shorter, sharper style, without embellishment of adjectives, to convey the terror struck into the people by the sound of the siren. Does it do this job?

What do YOU think? How would YOU handle it?

——————— o ———————

Thin shoulders hunched inside his anorak, Paul Freeland peered through the estate agent's window. Even in a monochrome photograph, the cottage looked so picturesque that the price displayed beneath it was incredibly low. Perhaps the place was riddled with dry rot, or death watch beetle, but Paul could not afford to be choosy; Angela's alimony left him short of cash and he needed somewhere to live – somewhere he could work in peace, without being bothered by other people. Was a little solitude too much for a man to ask?

Damn Angela, anyway. She was still an attractive woman. Why the hell didn't she get married again? A bitter smile twisted his lips as he told himself that no other man would be fool enough to marry a woman who possessed all the sensitivity of a steam-roller. He still winced when he recalled her scathing voice:

'Write a best-seller? You? Don't make me laugh. You're a hack, Paul, churning out the same old stuff year after year. Why don't you grow up?'

Comments: This is not a bad opening. It intrigues us by making us wonder why the price of the cottage is so low. The lively style stays well inside Freeland's viewpoint — everything is seen through his attitudes and prejudices.

However, since the rest of the story concerns a haunted mirror and has no connection with Freeland's failed marriage, and since the story was for a competition limited to 2000 words, the details about the wife and their relationship did not warrant the space they occupied. The writer decided to discard that aspect of the plot and in the finished version the wife wasn't mentioned at all.

——————— o ———————

The tropical sun beat down as the pretty blonde girl paced up and down her hotel room.

'But why, for heaven's sake, Jane?' She turned in anguish to her dark-haired companion, who was seated on the divan. 'Why did you send for them, of all people? You should know these folks don't work for nothing, and where are we to get extra money from?'

Jane fidgeted and stared at her pink fingernails. 'I'm sorry, Suzie, but I had to stop you worrying. I just wrote the blessed letter, and only stopped to think when the damage was done.' She was near to tears.

The blonde girl sighed and shook her head. 'Just like you, Fly-away Jane, but,' she put her arm round her sister, 'at least you did it from a good motive.' She settled back on the divan, then added, 'Oh, well, all we can do now is wait till they arrive. If they set off as soon as they got your letter they should be here soon.'

In the hotel lobby, the little Spanish hotelero swore loudly at an innoffensive monkey, who had just come in through the open window. The tiny animal hastily scampered out again and leapt to the branch of a palm tree, where he swung staring cheekily at the irate hotel-keeper. The Spaniard leant out of the window, still swearing the air blue, mainly because it gave him something to do on that hot sleepy afternoon.

He was brought back to his surroundings when a tall, muscular American tapped him on the shoulder. 'Hey, is this the Hotel Caramba?' he enquired in a deep-brown voice to suit his hair and eyes.

Comments: This is a little clumsy, though it does get us asking questions – Who are the girls? Who has Jane sent for, and why? The change of scene, from the hotel bedroom to the lobby, is a little soon and sudden – we're not sure yet who to identify with.

One wonders how much the writer really knows about Africa – it's not very convincing, is it? Is the word 'hotelero' a correct one?

However, when you know the writer is only fourteen years of age, this is actually a pretty good stab at the opening of a boy-meets-girl romance. Shows promise, I think. Do you agree?

———— o ————

It came about one Saturday evening, when Calum Izzard was sitting alone on the settle, with a pint of ale before him. As soon as he saw two strangers enter the Ale House, he knew they were not from 'these parts', by the cut of their tailored clothes, large clean white collars, and tall hats.

Together they strode through to where several smallholders were gathered around a blazing log fire. Calum recognised the voice of Ralph Rix. What was he saying?
'She came to my byre and tried to give my beast her herbs and remedies, and the cow went mad!'

'So did mine!' interrupted Seth Wier. 'The poor thing crashed into the door, and dropped down dead.'
'Aye,' said another. 'So did mine! I think she 'overlooked' the beasts. We should swim her in Pendle's Pond.'

It was obvious to Calum that the two strangers were Witch Finders. Suddenly, Calum felt inwardly cold. Didn't Ralph Rix ask his mother to tend his ailing cow last week? And Seth Wier, she visited his holding too. These men were plotting to prove that his mother was a witch. He listened some more. One of the strangers was speaking now.
'For the safety of the village people, we must 'swim her'. Let's get her! Where does she live?'

Comments: Shown here as the writer presented it, the layout of this tale needs reorganizing: line gaps between sections are not necessary since there's no change of scene, time or viewpoint; and paragraphs of dialogue should be indented just as others are.

Good points are the immediate use of dated language: It came about ... which tells us we're in history somewhere, as does the word settle and then the description of the clothes – just enough to be informative and create a picture of roughly when we are. Do we really need all those adjectives large clean white ... ? I'd have liked a little more description of the scene, a well-chosen word or two to tell me what an ale house of this period looked like, felt like, smelt like ...

The quotes round these parts struck me as odd; they draw attention to the fact that the author knows she's using a colloquial expression. Why is she ashamed of it? If this is meant to be from Calum's viewpoint, then the words are his and he would not put them in parenthesis. Did this strike an odd note for you, too? Does the same apply to overlooked, and to swim her (picked out in the final speech of this extract though not in the last line of the middle section!)? Whose quotes are they – the speaker's or the intruding author's? The latter, in my opinion; they should be removed. NB Had these phrases warranted being emphasized, they ought, of course, to have been framed by double quotes since they're already inside singles. The rule is: doubles inside singles, singles inside doubles, for definition. See earlier discussion on punctuation, in Chapter Two.

The second section, the conversation overheard, gets to the point a little too abruptly – witch-finders would surely tread warily when they first arrived. This could be dealt with by adding a sentence or two about some introductory chit-chat, before Calum's ears prick up when he hears what they're actually talking about.

In section three, verb tenses go a bit awry: it should be *Hadn't Ralph Rix asked his mother to tend his ailing cow last week? And Seth Wier, she had visited* ... Also, there should be another paragraph break after *witch*, because we move out of Calum's thoughts and back to what he's hearing.

———— o ————

Pete's first meeting with Jim Barnwell was as a result of his father's helping cousin Fred over a problem. Some time before that dreadful day when the Barnwells took over the Hedderton Manor, Bill had lent his nephew a horse, because his own had gone lame and was unable to finish the ploughing. After meeting Tom at the cricket match and agreeing that the grey gelding Shire in the stables was his and not part of the inventory, Bill had sent Pete to the farm to retrieve the animal, lest it should be sold.

Comments: This writer evidently holds, in his head, all the threads of his rather complicated tale and the varying relationships among the men, but he hasn't managed to convey them with much clarity, has he? Who is whose father, cousin, nephew? An added problem here is that the men all have short, ordinary, one-syllable names: Pete, Fred, Bill and Tom. Hard to differentiate one from t'other, isn't it?

Adding to the mix-up is the immediate flip (in sentence two) into flashback. *Some time before that dreadful day* . . . takes us a step back in time; this happens again in sentence three when we jump to a time *After* . . . *the cricket match*. So both the **who** and the **when** provide the reader with problems of confusion.

When writing a piece, whether fiction or non-fiction, you must have a clear idea of exactly what you're trying to convey, whose story it is and exactly *when* it's going to start. Don't leap-frog about – among characters *or* times – until your reader has a firm grasp of what's going on. Indeed, in a short story, if you can avoid flashbacks altogether, do so. While you're learning technique, it's far simpler for you, and your reader, if, like Alice, you begin at the beginning, go on until the end, then stop.

———— o ————

Edward edged the car slowly forward along the country lane that he had known as a youth, so very long ago. Memories shrouded in unhappiness were again flooding his thoughts, darkening his mood. He believed Time would have mellowed his memories, softening the misery of his youth, yet the bitterness was still smouldering, despite the years that had passed.

Comments: Brief as this extract is, it's over-written: the same thoughts (the passage of years between and the bitterness of his memories) are repeated in several different ways, bogging us down in unnecessary words. This particular passage could, to my mind, have been expressed in two sentences: *As Edward edged the car along the country lane, unhappy memories darkened*

his mood. He ought to have forgotten after so long, but the bitter-
ness was still smouldering.

That's enough to hook us and make us ask 'Why?' From there, the action should continue.

———————   o   ———————

'There was a heavy raid in Chesham last night, Miss Young,' the
grocer said to Aunt Freda as he skilfully folded a flat piece of stiff
blue paper to envelope two pounds of sugar. 'Did you hear it?'

'Yes, and as a result they turned up on my doorstep at three this
morning. They wanted me to look after these two toddlers while
their mother is in hospital,' she replied. 'I can't say no so long as
there's a bed for them.'

'How many youngsters have you got now?'

'Luckily there are only seven. After that raid yesterday I've got
two babies and two toddlers. Of course, I've still got my permanent
three.' Auntie nodded in our direction. Jim the eldest, Alec the
youngest, and I, were wondering at the Christmas tree standing at
the end of the shop. The branches were covered in glass chains
and birds, candles and tinsel, and tantalizing little parcels.

'I wish we could have a tree,' Alec whispered, looking unhappily
at Jim, who being the eldest was the one to whom we looked for
words of wisdom. Well, he was ten years old, after all.

Comments: This is a true story, but it still has to be shaped and crafted in order to read well. I've lost count of the number of students to whom I've made suggestions for improvement, only to have them cry, 'Oh, but it's true!' as if factuality is a guarantee of readability. True stories *can* make excellent raw material, but you can't simply throw them down on paper anyhow. It's 'the way you tell 'em' that counts.

This has a good, involving opening. Conversation gets us straight to the action; mention of 'the raid', followed by the grocer's making a sugar bag out of blue paper immediately tells us we're in a period setting – war-time. Then we meet 'the boys', and want to know who they are; why does Miss Young call them her 'permanent three'? The ingredients of under-privileged children, Christmas and war-time will have to be handled carefully so as not to get mawkish, but this has all the makings of a touching human story.

I advised this writer to consider tightening up the text a little by pruning some of the unnecessary words: I felt that Miss Young's first speech was a bit vague; who were the *they* who turned up on her doorstep? And for clarity the *she replied* ought to appear a little sooner. Also, the detail of which boy was oldest and which youngest is probably not necessary so soon – it can be brought out more subtly as the story progresses.

RECAP

- A good beginning is vital; it should interest, involve, and/or intrigue the reader at once.
- Include the five Ws.
- Even a true story has to be shaped.
- Try to avoid too early a foray into flashback.
- Be clear in your mind; then you'll be clear on the page.
- Remember that choice of sentence structure, length, and even the printed shape of words can affect the mood of your piece.

Exercise: Look now at your own story-opening. From what you've learned, do you think it could be improved in any way?

Try it. Or write a new, better one.

6 · Credible Characters
From a Handful of Dust . . .

Who are they?

A story is about people – characters – and the writer's task is to bring them to life on the page. I'm often asked if I use people from real life as actors in my stories: the answer is, basically, no. You can take certain characteristics of real people but, as true life stories have to be crafted to make good reading, so people have to be shaped to make good fictional characters. They seldom transfer well from street to page without radical surgery.

One thing that doesn't alter, however, is human emotion. Love, hatred, greed, revenge, and the rest, fire all people from the Stone Age to the far future. Use emotion to lend fire to your characters, to give them purpose. A nicely balanced story will include many different emotions.

Your actors can be human, alien, animal, even mechanical, but Martin the Martian, the rabbits of Watership Down, Thomas the Tank Engine *et al* are given human characteristics – anthropomorphized, to use the technical term – because readers need to identify with them. Whatever species they might be, the same rules of good fiction apply.

I name this child . . .

One of the easiest ways to make your characters begin to live is to **name** them. Daphne du Maurier's *Rebecca*, where the narrating heroine is never named or described, is one of those exceptions which prove the rule. As you assign names to your actors, their identities begin to take shape in your mind, flesh coalescing around a skeleton. They may emerge from your imagination already bearing names; if they do, trust your subconscious and let them be who they are. For others, you might search through long lists of names before you find the right one.

Finding exactly the right name is more important than might appear at first sight. The name has to fit the character, his background, the time he lives in and the role he has to play. Beware of anachronisms: a seventeenth-century girl, for instance, would not be called Wendy – that name was first coined by J. M. Barrie. Conversely, erudite modern parents might well choose to bless their child with some historical name – Daedalus, say. If you decide on an unusual name for your main character, it may look quirky, but perhaps you're writing a quirky book, so it fits. Consider Mervyn Peake's *Titus Groan*, where we meet Lord Sepulchrave and his daughter Lady Fuchsia, not to mention Doctor Prunesquallor. In more realistic fiction, you might employ a striking name for a character who does not appear frequently. A lady named Hermione Harmistead had a vital role to play in one of my books. She was a relatively minor character, but each time she appeared her memorable name acted as a label to remind the reader of her identity.

Since a plethora of unusual names can create a comic effect, 'classic' names are preferable for your main players. Ring the changes with them; make some short and some long, and use as many different initial letters as you can – Pat and Christopher, William and Beryl. The *look* of the name – the shape of the word on the page – is even more important than the sound: Max and May could do well in a radio play, where they're spoken aloud, but on paper they could easily be confused; if you introduce Willy, Milly, Billy, Wally, Sally and Polly, your reader will never sort out who's which; avoid having Tim, Tom, Ted, Jim and Jed combine too often in your pages, likewise Mr Forster, Mrs Forrest and old Forsyte.

Relatively speaking

You might find a family tree helpful, not necessarily for publication (though some readers of long, complicated novels find them useful). Figuring out who is related to whom, when they were born, how old they were when they married, and when they had their children, could furnish ideas for sub-plots. One such tree produced for me a family in which twins* began to appear: this became an integral part of the subsequent plot. In another, a young girl married a much older man: he had delayed long before marrying, said my imagination, because he was homosexual. I decided to make him impotent, too, poor chap; so the children of the marriage became a result of the mother's extramarital dalliance, which gave me enormous scope for drama when the truth came out. None of that was in my mind when I sat down to sketch out the family tree, but it made a useful plot twist.

It's great fun playing God!

---

* A quick note about twins: the mistaken-identity plot has been done to death. Avoid it, unless you can come up with a really original twist.

So, what did he look like?

Descriptive writing is a vital part of prose, which is why it has its own section later in this book. But, on the subject of characters, the need to include *physical* descriptions, especially details of facial features, depends on what kind of story you're writing. A short story set in modern times, among familiar surroundings, calls for minimal description − and anyway long descriptive tracts are out of place in most short stories. Keep longer passages for novels, when you have more space to colour in your picture and when you want your reader to see the characters more clearly, but always remember to mix description in among the action and dialogue, to keep the story flowing.

Gloria burst into the room in distress. She was a slender young woman some twenty years old, wearing fashionably slit jeans and a striped red and white T-shirt, with long dark hair trailing down her shoulders and tears bursting from her hazel eyes. 'Oh, Allan! It's the baby.'

Her husband leapt to his feet, a stocky young man in a sweatshirt embroidered with the logo of a pop group, baggy sackcloth trousers and bare feet. He had very short hair of a mousey hue. Staring at Gloria with an anxious expression on his round, florid face, he said, 'Danny? Why, what . . .'

Can you see how, here, pauses for physical description only interrupt the narrative? Is it vital to bombard your reader with these details? If, instead, we simply write:

Gloria burst into the room in distress. 'Oh, Allan! It's the baby!' 'Danny?' He leapt to his feet. 'Why, what . . .'

Now, we're immediately plunged into the drama of the story. What they look like doesn't really matter yet. If you want to give your readers a picture, you slip it in with phrases such as:

pulling fretfully at her long dark hair; *she looked suddenly childlike and vulnerable in her slit jeans and T-shirt*; *swore violently, clutching his bare foot — he'd forgotten Danny's toy train on the floor.* These help to fill out the picture but *at the same time* continue the action.

For unusual settings, foreign countries or historical times, you'll need to say more about the way characters look because your readers won't be so familiar with details of clothes and hairstyles. If you're writing romance, then again you need to be more specific since romance readers like to know what colour hair and eyes the man and girl have. HE will always be tall and strong: SHE must be shorter, and slim. But it's not necessary to describe every single feature, even if that were possible. Your reader will have personal taste in beauty, both male and female, so sketch in the basics and let her take it from there, visualizing her own ideal.

For less gorgeous characters, a well-chosen phrase giving an overall impression is effective: *he was lined and gnarled, like an ancient apple tree*; *she had a face like a pelican*; *a plump girl in white cycling shorts that showed every dimple of cellulite*; *a dog named Rags, who resembled a dishmop.*

The author must carefully choose exactly *which* characters to describe in great detail, which to sketch in and which to leave as a 'type' — the maid, the taxi driver. If you say too much about walk-on players, they will stick in the reader's mind and he will expect them to reappear and have some connection with the plot.

The only time you need to go into fine detail is when that detail is relevant to the plot. Your murderer may have a wooden leg and you plan for this to provide a vital clue, so you draw your reader's attention to it, obviously or subtly, whichever suits your purpose. By obviously, I mean you describe the defect clearly; more subtly, you would mention it in passing so as not to make it too obvious. What you do *not* do is fail to mention it at all until the revelatory moment at the end: *Good heavens, Sanders has a wooden leg – that explains the peculiar footsteps we heard!* I know that Agatha Christie broke this rule in *The Murder of Roger Ackroyd*, where the narrator turned out to be the murderer, too: he simply glossed over the facts that might have given him away. But that's akin to telling a shaggy dog story. In my opinion, it's cheating your reader! Don't do it.

Make them human – make them fallible

The most noble and heroic characters can be made more human, and often more appealing, by giving them a flaw of some kind. After all, none of us is perfect, physically or otherwise: the most memorable heroine could be selfish, or forgetful, or thoughtless (think of Scarlett O'Hara, who was far from perfect). A top model may bite her nails: a small scar may mar (or make) a man's handsome features. How does the fact that she bites her nails affect her – is she bitterly ashamed or does she shrug it off and wear false nails? Suppose she then tries for a job advertising hand cream . . . How did the man come by the scar? The answer can reveal more about his character: maybe he was injured saving someone's life (what a hero!) or maybe he was cut by a knife (far more sinister!). Who was holding the knife? When, why, how . . . ? Exploring such questions will add extra dimensions to your plot.

The iceberg

You should know a good deal more about your characters than will ever go on the page. Their background is like the iceberg: not much of it shows, but the hidden part is in the writer's mind and gives the story weight and balance. Establish your players' ages fairly soon. Their occupations will also give the reader clues, as will their taste in decor and the things with which they choose to surround themselves.

As in real life, outside events, family influences and genetic traits must have shaped your fictional people. Some of these will be very subtle, hardly mentioned though known to you; others can be of major importance. To illustrate, in one of my romantic suspense novels the denouement had the heroine trapped, with a forest on fire around her. Naturally, the hero was due to arrive like the seventh cavalry. However, to add a little extra emotional impact, I made him terrified of fire. But how had he acquired that fear? Because, I decided, when he was small, his mother had been burned to death when their house went up in flames. The novel began with that flashback scene, the small boy being carried forcibly away from the house where he could hear his mother screaming. The reader wasn't told exactly which of the men this had happened to, but as the main plot developed we saw Neil speak sharply to his sister when she was careless with fire; later, during a car rally, he was unable to drive through smoke from burning stubble (before stubble-burning was banned, of course). So, by the time the heroine was on the point of being roasted, my readers, and the girl, understood what courage – what depth of feeling – it took for Neil to rescue her.

Exit left, chased by a bear . . .

Your characters need to have a life even off the page: they existed before the story began and will continue to do so after you write The End – unless they all start out as babies and end up dead. They will also, unless they're cardboard cut-outs, do and say things when they're not actually on-stage in your scenes. Make sure you let them live in this way – you, their creator, should know what they've been doing while they were absent. It could well be important to the plot.

I once saw a play, a courtroom mystery, where everything hinged on the housekeeper's evidence. This was contrived so that, while telling the truth as she knew it, she damned her employer as his wife's murderer. Unfortunately, in order to believe this was probable, one had to accept that the woman overheard only the very worst moments of her employers' relationship; never eavesdropped on happy times; and never discussed any of it with the wife. Considering that she appeared to share a close, confiding relationship with her mistress, she must have been incredibly stupid not to detect that the marriage was, in fact, a deeply caring one.

What the author had done was to write as if the housekeeper had no existence except on stage, in the scenes that were enacted for us, and that no conversations took place other than those we were allowed to hear. The premise was so implausible that I wondered how on earth the play ever came to be produced. The answer was, I guess, the celebrity author. That name alone guaranteed an audience, whatever the quality of the play.

Those of us who cannot (yet!) command an audience by our name alone have to be a bit more careful when conceiving characters.

Body language

People give away their inner feelings by the way they hold themselves, or move, or with sidelong glances. People who are ashamed of bad teeth, or fearful of bad breath, reveal the fact by constantly putting a hand to their mouth; downcast eyes might mean modesty or calculated coyness; folded arms (a keep-off signal) reveal aggression, or hurt, or perhaps a teenage girl's embarrassment over her budding breasts. So body language provides another tool for the writer's workbox.

How does your character enter a room? A confident person will stride in, head high, smiling ... A shy person may slip round the door and merge with the crowd unobserved ... A self-conscious person may be so anxious not to be seen that she creates havoc by taking the most direct route across a restaurant, sending drinks flying and waiters scattering ... You can probably think of other examples, any one of which will be far more interesting than saying, 'Wilbur crossed to the window.' How I hate that phrase: it tells me nothing except that the person moved. *How* did he move, for goodness' sake? Did he limp, stride, shuffle, amble, dawdle ... ? Our language is full of wonderful descriptive verbs. Use them, please!

In your first drafts you may well find you use flat, uninspired language. That's normal – we all do it. But, when you're editing, notice it, and alter it. Small moments in your narrative can serve to illuminate character, draw a sharper picture, raise questions, add tension, all of which help to widen the reader's comprehension.

Add the unexpected

People are not always predictable. The mildest peacemaker may be pushed to anger, or a seemingly prim person may swear. Naturally, however much of a surprise this may be to the reader, you, the author, must know exactly why it happens and should supply plausible explanations. Don't simply create a situation because it's going to make good drama, if it doesn't fit with the character. Australian soap opera writers cheat like this a lot of the time: their characters are puppets who alter with the whims of each successive crisis, which is what makes such programmes so unreal and lightweight. As *your* story progresses, let your characters grow, develop, let them learn from the experiences you put them through, as real people do. They change while remaining true to their own nature. If you doubt this, think of your own family and friends.

No two people react in exactly the same way to a given stimulus, either. A woman finds a body, or sees a mouse . . . Does she, inevitably, scream? She does? Bor-ing! Cliché! Or say a girl in a bikini wiggles by . . . Does every man leer and lust after her? Wouldn't your chap be a more interesting type if he didn't react in that knee-jerk way? By creating a non-cliché response, and inventing good motivation for it, you reveal a lot about the character and make your writing more original.

Naked, and ye clothed me . . .

As with descriptions of physical appearance, **clothes** are best described either briefly or not at all, so long as they fall within the accepted norm. Everyone knows what *jeans and a T-shirt* look like, so if your heroine throws them on in a hurry you need say no more; a crowd of contemporary teenagers will probably be dressed in their street-cred outfits of baggy, untidy clothes, long, untidy hair and enormous ugly shoes (seen from my middle-aged viewpoint, of course). But an eccentric way of dressing – a touch of the dandy, a trace of the slattern – can tell a lot about your character. Go into detail only where attire deviates from the usual, *and*, of course, where it adds something to the rest of the story – where it's relevant.

Let's imagine that one of those teenage girls is wearing a gold necklace; you can't simply mention it and leave it, it must have a *reason* for being there. Perhaps the girl has stolen it, and is about to be arrested; perhaps she's been left it by her grandmother and, underneath her outward show of bravado, she is grieving bitterly; or does she have a wealthy boyfriend who has given her a necklace and made her pregnant, so that she's worrying how to tell her family – or is she casually planning an abortion? In any of these cases, the necklace is a means of revealing a great deal about the girl's nature. If it has no such story-significance, don't zoom in on it, don't even mention it. Realize that *by drawing attention to anything you raise the reader's expectations.*

Giving themselves away

Far better than your describing them, allow your characters to reveal *themselves*, by what they do and the way they do it. Our old friend Cassandrina Dustworthy writes *Emily kept her home neat and tidy*, when she could have said, *Emily had taken only one sip of her tea before a crease in one of her cushions demanded that she leap up again to smooth it*, or something similar. It's more interesting to *show* the person behaving in character rather than baldly (and boringly) *telling* what kind of person s/he is. As we already know, though, in 'The Christmas Present' Emily's neatness isn't relevant; so let's not waste words on it.

If your central player is an untidy scatterbrain of a girl, rather than writing *Donna was an untidy scatterbrain* try something like: *Donna dashed into the flat, tripped over the cord of the vacuum cleaner and just saved herself from landing headlong in the pile of dirty linen overflowing from its basket. Where was that letter? Ah, yes – in the kitchen, among the clutter of unwashed dishes.* Now we can see for ourselves what sort of a girl Donna is – she has revealed herself as people do in life, by what she does and how she does it; we can also see her flat, and we're intrigued to know what the letter is about. Aren't we?

'Telling' in this way takes up more space, so it needs close scrutiny. Does it add something essential to our knowledge of the character? If not – if it's just a piece of writing for writing's sake – excise it ruthlessly.

Keeping notes

You might try keeping a notebook on your characters, in order to build up a word-picture for yourself in the planning stages and also to note extra details while the piece is in progress. Jot down any idea that comes to you. It may not all go into the finished manuscript; some of it may be altered, or discarded – that doesn't matter. Include name, date of birth, physical details of build and colouring, personal habits, likes and dislikes, faults and virtues, and anything else that will make this person a rounded individual in your mind. Only cartoon characters are entirely bad or entirely good: even a serial murderer may feed the birds, enjoy a symphony, or be kind to his mother.

A page taken at random from one of my own notebooks reads: **Lady Maud Fyncham**, *b 1853, older than her husband. Plain, v tall, pale, angular. Haughty, peremptory with servants and friends alike. Chestnut hair. Likes riding, breeds horses. Taut planes on chiselled face. No spare flesh. Fine white skin but cheeks blemished by broken veins, lips thin and eyes buried in bony sockets. A bit butch, uninterested in sex except for procreation. Adored her son but can't take to her daughter.*
Bella, *her daughter, b 1886. Spoiled; long, straight ginger hair. Grey eyes like father. Pointed, bad-tempered face. Birthday Sept 10.* (Her actual birthday became important to the plot, so I jotted it down as a reminder.)

Other, more major, characters have more detailed notes, still others merit only a line or two. These notes grow longer as the book progresses and you add more information, such as faults and prejudices, habits of speech or manner, the age the person was when some traumatic event happened, or where they were at the time.

Notice that I memoed even small details such as the colour of hair. It's always worthwhile writing down this information, especially for characters who are not on stage all the time. You'd be surprised how many authors create characters whose eyes and hair alter dramatically and inexplicably. Even lost limbs — a leg blown off in a sea-battle, an arm surgically removed — have been known to grow back, to be used a chapter or two later, without character or author mentioning the miracle.

In the back of such notebooks, I jot down other details as they enter the story — names of houses, dogs and horses, walk-on characters and so forth. Then, when I need to refer to them again and have probably forgotten what name I chose, the notebook saves me from having to plough through an entire manuscript to find one word!

Carelessness over detail does not impress a commissioning editor and it's the stuff of copy-editors' nightmares. Don't expect your editor to do your work for you. You, who created these people, must know them more intimately than you know your own family.

A sketch-map of your fictional setting might be a help, too. Exactly how far is it from A to B? Does the house face east to the sunrise or west to the evening sky? What kind of terrain lies between house and inn, village and town? Working out such details helps get your imagination going.

To sum up, in many areas of character drawing, the deviation is more telling than the norm. What your actor does, or wears, or thinks, or looks like, different from the general standard, is what makes him individual. Don't give every single character a tic, a stammer or a wooden leg, or you'll risk turning your piece into comedy, but an oddity here and there helps bring a story to life and can make a player memorable.

Examples

The following extracts are examples of descriptive character drawing. The longer ones come from novels, the shorter ones from short stories, demonstrating the different approaches you need for each. Short stories should be spare, tightly written, every word having a purpose. Novels need more depth, more layers of characterization and plot, so naturally you include more information. Novels are not, however, short stories padded out to fill more pages. Each sentence should still do its work. See if the examples fulfil this function. Note that there's not much dialogue – we shall come to dialogue in the next chapter.

As you read the extracts, remember the points made above and ask yourself – what is the writer trying to achieve? Is the writing effective? Over-written or under-written? If *you* were doing it, how would you improve it? If it works well, *why* does it do so, and *how*?

———— o ————

The first example demonstrates how the aforementioned Lady Maud Fyncham enters the story (*A Child of Secrets*, Headline, 1993). It's not the *only* way of doing it; it's not the *best* way (there's no such thing as the 'best way' to write): no, this is simply the way *I* did it, in this particular book.

It is 1891 and Jess (the main, VP character) has been summoned to the big house . . .

Against the southern window, framed against the flare of daylight outside, a woman lounged on the window-board, staring out as if watching for something.

Jess made a curtsey. The movement seemed to distract Lady Fyncham, who glanced round, perused Jess in silence for a moment, then turned away, saying, 'My daughter is five years old. How old were your last charges?'

Charges? Jess puzzled over the word. Did it mean her brothers and sisters? 'Well, milady . . . There was Sam – he's now twelve. Joe was . . . eight years old last April. And there was the baby.' She was going to add that baby Sarah May had died before she was two, but Lady Fyncham wasn't listening. Lady Fyncham was impatiently watching for something beyond the window.

Remembering the letter Reverend Clare had written, Jess fumbled for it in her bag. 'There's this, milady. My reference.'

'H'm? Oh, yes. Well, bring it here, girl.' She clicked her fingers and Jess, shaking with nerves, forced her feet to cross the thick carpet.

Close to, Lady Maud Fyncham was an impressive woman with a taut, chiselled face. She hadn't an ounce of spare flesh on her. Her skin was fine and white to go with that rich chestnut hair, but broken veins blemished her cheeks, and her thin lips looked mean. Having received the letter, she waved Jess back with a peremptory hand, tore open the envelope and scanned the contents.

'Reverend Clare seems to think you'll do,' she said, and, 'Ah! Good!' as a movement outside drew her attention. A groom was leading a horse up to the iron railing and through the gate. The horse seemed unsettled, unnerved by the wind, tossing its head and dancing sideways, but the sight of it made Lady Fyncham smile a tight smile and get to her feet, swirling the skirt of her riding habit to one side. The skirt was split to the waist. Beneath it she wore mannish breeches and high, polished boots.

Vaguely shocked at such unladylike attire, Jess stared up at her prospective employer. The squire's wife was very tall – Jess hardly came as high as her shoulder. Snatching up a riding crop from the writing desk, she strode across the room and tugged at an embroidered bell-pull with a silken tassel. 'I suggest you make arrangements with Nanny. If Reverend Clare thinks you'll do, that's good enough for me. You'll get the usual pay – whatever that is. You can start as soon as you like. Tell the girl to take you up to the nursery suite. I have business to attend to.' With which, she swept out.

I've used quite a bit of detail in the physical description because, Lady Maud being an important part of the story, I wanted my reader to see her clearly at this first meeting – through Jess's eyes, of course. Lady Maud's words and actions reveal the kind of person she is. At least, I hope they do. What do you think? Is it effective?

——————— o ———————

Meet Etta, who suffers from agoraphobia and is trying to get up the courage to go through the dreaded door:

Etta sat transfixed in her chair. She looked as immaculate as ever in her navy blue dress and matching shoes. The new addition to her wardrobe completed her outfit. The charcoal grey coat fitted her perfectly. Unmoving, she sat with her eyes firmly fixed on the door before her.

The emotion here is nicely suggested, but the rest is rather muddled, the first and last sentences at odds with the rest. She has dressed in her best in order to bolster her courage – fine. But exactly what is the *new addition to her wardrobe* – dress, shoes, or coat? – and is it relevant? How can she look *immaculate in her navy dress* if she's wearing a charcoal grey coat over it? And to whose eyes does she look immaculate?

Can you suggest how it might be improved?

——————— o ———————

This paragraph comes from a story about a down-and-out 'bag lady':

She placed another piece of frost-covered wood into her trolley. The knaws and knots of the wood resembled her weather-worn fingers. The cold affected them badly. The fingerless black gloves offered little protection against the biting winter chill of early morning. She was thankful for the thick woollen socks and zip-up fur lined ankle boots she had been given at the refuge as she made her way along the river's edge towards the underpass. She pulled up the frayed collar of her chequered coat tighter round her neck. The glare of the sun caused her eyes to water.

Again, the atmosphere and feeling are well imagined, but not expressed in the best way. Being really picky, I can't find the word *knaw* in my dictionaries, though both 'knag' and 'knar' are there, meaning 'a knot in wood', so this word is tautological. We could cut the adjectives *zip-up* (unnecessary detail), and *winter* (repetitive, we already have *frost-covered*, *cold*, and *biting chill*). The phrase *as she made her way along . . .* is misplaced, because she obviously hadn't been given the clothes as she made her way along the river bank.

Not least, the rhythm needs variety. We have six sentences here: three begin with 'The'; three begin with 'She', and all of them are flat statements, led by the main clause. When editing, the author should try to vary this.

It could be edited to read: *As she fumbled another piece of frost-covered kindling into her trolley, she noticed how the knotted wood resembled her fingers. Her arthritic hands ached, fingerless gloves giving little protection against the biting chill of early morning. She was thankful, though, for the thick woollen socks and fur-lined ankle boots that the people at the refuge had given her. Pulling up the frayed collar of her chequered coat, eyes watering from the glare of the rising sun, she started along the river's edge towards the underpass.*

Six sentences become four, two of which start with subordinate clauses: *As she . . .* and *Pulling up . . .* At the beginning, I've changed *placed* to *fumbled*, which is more descriptive considering her aching, arthritic hands. Study other small changes, too. Can you see why I made them? Would you do the same? This rewrite also gives an **easier transition**, with her moving out of this paragraph into whatever happens in the next.

——————— o ———————

Now, something completely different. Here's Lucy Cary, around 1814, taken by night to a gloomy mansion where she meets her grandmother, the Countess Helena Kalinskaya, for the first time:

'Here she is, ma'am – Miss Cary,' the housekeeper announced, and swept out, leaving Lucy alone with the eerie shadows and the awful smell that nearly choked her.

Peering into darkness that seemed to gather around one particular corner of the room, Lucy discerned a low couch and a figure which sat there. As her eyes adjusted to the dimness, she was shocked to make out the shape of a tall powdered wig. Faint candlelight gleamed on scarlet satin and a hand rested on the arm of the couch, all skin and bone, curled like a claw, bearing a ring with a huge red stone.

'I can't see you,' the woman rasped. 'Bring a candle.'

Trembling with both fascination and horror, Lucy fetched one of the candlesticks, carrying it carefully with one hand guarding the flame. Its light showed her the spectacle of an aged woman dressed in the costume of forty years before, a panniered skirt and low-necked bodice against which a wrinkled bosom swelled obscenely, aided by tight corseting. The sickly scent emanated from her, a mixture of old perfumes and stale body odours. But it was the face that unnerved Lucy most – a face raddled with age and small-pox scars, painted thickly with dead-white powder and dotted with beauty patches, some round and some crescent-shaped; lips made a bright red slash in the mask, with eyes sunken and balefully peering out beneath a high, lavishly curled wig clotted with powder.

Not exactly your sweet old-fashioned granny, is she? That, of course, is why she's painted in such detail – because she *is* unusual. We are meant to share Lucy's revulsion. Note the way this is achieved, by choice of words: *eerie shadows, awful smell, hand like a claw, wrinkled bosom swelled obscenely, sickly scent, stale body odours, raddled, scars, dead-white, mask, balefully* . . . Does the writing achieve its object of turning the old woman into a horror?

Another point to ponder, on costume – although the ancient Countess takes it to extremes, older people do tend to cling to the fashions of their younger days and have probably always done so. Back in history, not everyone dressed in the height of fashion, though if you look at books of costume reference you might think that they did. In truth, only the very rich could afford to dress fashionably all the time. In country areas the fashions tended to be delayed by months or even years, and poorer people had to make do in various ways, with hand-me-downs, or make-it-yourselves.

——————— o ———————

Another short story begins:

Charles Danvers stepped out into the dark, damp evening, his face grim. It had been raining heavily for most of the day but had now slowed to a steady drizzle. Pausing in the shelter of the doorway, he took a deep breath, welcoming the cold night air into his lungs. With a slight shiver he pulled up the collar of his coat and ran splashing through the puddles to his car. As he switched on the ignition, the green light of the digital clock on the dashboard flashed eight o'clock. He should have been home by now, though Barbara wouldn't be worried tonight, only impatient for his return. With a deep sigh, he pulled out of the car park and began the long drive home.

Another good one, establishing mood and atmosphere, raising questions in our minds. Why is he grim-faced? Why will his wife be waiting impatiently but not worriedly? The author might consider fine-tuning by cutting out the second sentence: we already know the evening is damp and the puddles through which Danvers splashes tell us it has been raining heavily, so that second sentence can be dispensed with.

Note that we aren't told what Danvers looks like, because it doesn't matter. He's a male figure in the darkness and the rain, wearing a coat – that's sufficient, for now.

What did *you* think of it?

——————— ○ ———————

How about this?

He was a kindly looking man, fiftyish with piercing blue eyes, immaculately dressed in a dark grey suit, plain white shirt and a club tie, not a bit as Jim had imagined him. Knowing his awesome reputation, he had expected to meet some wild-eyed psychopath.

This is not bad, though it's a bit clichéd with *piercing blue* eyes and *immaculately dressed*; the *awesome reputation* is rather vague (awesome in what way?); it could be meant as a hook, but it would work just as well without the adjective. I also feel that the second sentence might be better put first. We could tidy it up thus: *Knowing the man's reputation, Jim had expected to meet some wild-eyed psychopath. Instead, he saw a kindly man, fiftyish, with vivid blue eyes, dressed in immaculate grey suit, plain white shirt and club tie.*

Slightly better, do you think? I still feel it's too heavy on the adjectives — I count ten of them in these three lines. Or are they all necessary to give us a clear picture of this man? Would *conservatively dressed* have been enough for his clothes?

Feel free to argue.

RECAP

- Choose your characters' names with care and discretion.
- Drawing up a family tree could add unexpected twists.
- Study body language and mannerisms to add realism.
- Keep them human — give them faults and foibles.
- Remember that they exist *off the page*, too.
- Keep a notebook of facts about them.
- Let your players reveal *themselves*, by word and deed.

Having built your iceberg of background information, choose judiciously *exactly how much* needs to show on the page in your particular piece.

Constantly ask yourself: **Is it relevant?**

Exercise: Create a character. Choose from:
   a) The hero of a tough adventure story
   b) A teenaged single mother for a short story with a moral
   c) The middle-aged main character of a story about triumph over apparent failure
   d) The heroine of a sexy romance

Give this person an appropriate name. Make notes on background, appearance and personality. Decide what virtue, and what compatible flaw, you're going to give her/him.

Now, invent some reason, appropriate to the type of story, for the person to visit a hotel (remember there are all kinds of hotel, from the sumptuous to the flea-ridden); then imagine yourself in the lobby of this hotel, either as an unseen observer or as a participant in the action, when your character comes in. Write what happens.

Don't play safe, let your imagination run wild. You may surprise yourself.

7 · Dialogue
– Let Them Speak for Themselves

Who's speaking, please?

'What's this chapter about?'

   'I assume it's concerned with dialogue.'

   'Dialogue? You mean, people talking to each other?'

   'Yes, quite. People talking. As we're doing.'

   'What, you and me? Is this dialogue, then?'

   'Of course.'

   'Blimey! And I thought we were just having a chinwag. Well, what do you know? Dialogue, eh? Fancy that!'

   'Actually, I could fancy a pint a good deal more readily.'

   'Now you're talking!'

This duologue illustrates what you can do with pure speech, devoid of all narrative, even 'he said'. Despite that, did you begin to get a feeling of what gender these characters were, what age, and from what background? They were different types, weren't they? What makes you think so?

Dialogue has several functions to perform. It reveals character, gives information, discloses (or conceals) thoughts, adds description, builds suspense, raises a smile . . . It can also point up relationships between characters: a man may be bombastic with his brow-beaten wife, unsure with his sarcastic boss. But, whatever else, dialogue must **add something** to the story, so that narrative flow continues.

If you have a thesaurus, see how many variations it gives for the verb 'said': *spoke, mentioned, uttered, declared, whispered, prattled, gabbled, gushed, stammered, raved* ... The list is long. (If you *don't* have a thesaurus, put one on your birthday list.) However, before you assault your bookshelf in order to find other examples, let me point out that, most of the time, your reader doesn't even bother to read these verbs — he notices mainly the words enclosed by the quotes. In the introduction to this chapter, since only two people were involved, 'he said' and 'he replied' and 'Tom answered', etc., would have been extraneous, don't you think? 'He expostulated', 'he riposted', 'Tom averred' might have added to the comedy, but in most cases such ornamented language looks affected. So why bother? When dialogue is flowing, use the verbs of **saying** only as signposts for your reader.

Incidentally, avoid using too many non-vocal verbs as adjuncts with dialogue: *'Hello,' he grinned*; *'If you want,' she shrugged*; *'All right,' he nodded*. You may get away with an occasional eccentricity of this kind, but actually each of these examples comprises two sentences, which should be separated: *'Hello.' He grinned*. You could, maybe, express it *She shrugged: 'Hello'*, but even that's debatable. Why not be right? Try *He said with a grin*; *She replied, shrugging*; or *He nodded. 'All right.'* All of these are good grammatical English.

Which leads us on to another method of indicating who's speaking, as well as indicating mood and movement. Try using pieces of *narrative* before or after a line of dialogue:

Tom shifted in his seat, avoiding her eyes. 'I was only talking to the woman. What makes you think . . .' Putting this together in one paragraph tells us that Tom is the speaker. The narrative also implies, from his body language, that he's lying, doesn't it? You wouldn't need to add 'he said evasively', because it's already there in the context.

The tone and meaning should, ideally, be implicit in the spoken words. I hope you could 'hear' the voices of the two people in the introduction, without my having to tell you *how* the words were said. Occasionally the verb is vital, as when the tone of voice is unexpected: *'I love you!' she yelled.* Or maybe, *'If you do that again, I shall hit you,' his mother cooed.* As I mentioned earlier, choose a strong verb in preference to a weak verb embellished by an adverb. Here 'cooed' is better than 'said sweetly'.

Each of your players should have a unique voice, i.e. 'way of saying things': his own vocabulary, her special way of using imagery. Let your sailor use references to the sea; a housewife may employ archaeological allusions (she's studying the subject at night school) or have horizons no wider than the next meal, last night's TV, or the school holidays; a merchant banker will use professional business jargon, but may also have his mind on his golf handicap/his new car/his disabled son.

Verbal habits add individuality, too – take note of those you hear around you: some people swear every other word or two; some say 'you know?'; or 'as I said to Harry', or 'I mean to say . . .' Listen and you'll hear them doing it. Make notes. Use these verbal idiosyncrasies to enliven your writing (not *all* the time, of course: employ them like garlic – with discretion, as flavouring).

Consider, too, that people do not always say what they mean. Conversations are frequently elliptical, talking all round the subject without getting to the nub, creating endless opportunities for misunderstanding. Dialogue should illustrate this aspect of human behaviour while avoiding being too obtuse or tedious. Often the characters are saying one thing while your narrative is hinting at the truth lying beneath, which heightens dramatic impact for your reader. Sometimes they downright lie to each other. In fact, a great deal of what we say is designed to create an effect, to conceal the full truth. An outright lie, a diplomatic untruth, an evasion, a terminological inexactitude . . .

Here's a piece from my book *The Clouded Land* (Headline, 1994). The scene takes place in 1911, involving the heroine, Kate (first person VP narrator), with her cousin Emmet, whom she's just met:

The place was known as the sanctum, which, as Emmet loftily informed me, was short for, 'Sanctum sanctorum – that's Latin. It means—'

'Holy of holies,' said I.

Emmet stared, blue eyes bright beneath a soft forelock of golden hair. 'You know Latin?'

I shrugged. 'A little.' I didn't tell him how little.

Emmet was at Cambridge – the only one of the family to have achieved such scholarship. He liked to show off about it and was particularly condescending to me and to his sister 'Toria' – he called her that to annoy his mother. We were, after all, mere girls, and not expected to have brains.

Because I enjoyed seeing his eyes widen with utter amazement, I added, 'I'm hoping to go to college – the London School of Economics. Didn't anyone tell you? That's one reason I came to England.' My parents had held out the chance of that college place like a carrot to a donkey, and it was a tempting prospect, a measure of independence that might lead to other openings. 'As a matter of fact, I was offered a place at Berlin University' – that made him stare! – 'but Pa, my stepfather, didn't approve. He's old-fashioned. He thinks women should be kept back, with no right to a place in the world as equal—' Realizing I was on my high horse, I stopped myself.

'You're a suffragette!' Emmet exclaimed, partly horrified and partly admiring.

'Yes,' said I with a lift of my chin. 'I believe I am. I can drive, too. And I've smoked a cigarette. Fearfully modern of me, what?'

Later, I regretted my moment of hubris. At the dinner table, Emmet merrily informed the company that they had a dangerous subversive in their midst, at which every eye turned balefully on me, as if I were a black beetle that had suddenly crawled on to the food.

Kate's annoyance makes her boastful. Hubris is not normally a fault of hers, but she's goaded into it. And then she pays for it, which adds dramatic irony and gives the conversation extra relevance, carrying the story along. We learn a little about Emmet, too, and we're briefly reminded what he looks like. But we see him through Kate's perceptions; *she* is the VP character, the first person narrator. All we know of Emmet's thoughts and attitudes is what Kate assumes, and her assumptions *could* be wrong.

In life, we only truly know what's going on in our own mind (if then). When writing fiction, we can illuminate several sides of an argument by showing, or implying, what each character is feeling. But, whatever they say, whether they're angry, evasive, sick as a moon or over the parrot with delight, what they say should always be **true to character**.

Look closely at the construction of the dialogue between Kate and Emmet, at where the narrative comes, what it tells you, and which verbs of saying are used. There's no 'right' or 'wrong' way to do these things: the question is, does the piece fulfil the tasks it has been set?

Dialect: bootiful, really bootiful!

As to use of **dialect**, opinions vary. Some advocate a free rein; others advise caution; still others say you shouldn't attempt to reproduce local accents at all. My own advice would be to use dialect sparingly, giving only a flavour. Great tracts of phonetic spelling are difficult to follow, as you will know if your local paper prints pieces in broad shire-speak: brief though they are, they take an hour to decipher. It's far better, for our purposes, to add a hint of local speech rather than weary your reader by forcing him to work out what 'oo ar, me owld tiddy-oggy, that's reet gradely' is supposed to mean.

Try decoding this: *'Hare's sum towills. Git yew naow droi woil oi foind suthin' fer yew tew wayer, moi booty. Thet'll hev tew be whatsomiver oi can foind, moind. There hen't been no young lay- dies in this hare howse, not fer minny a long yare, that there hen't.'*

Difficult to follow? Probably not very accurate, either. Since everyone has his own idea of how dialect should be phoneti- cally presented, you're bound to offend somebody. Wouldn't it have been better to write: *'Here's some towels. Get you now dry while I find somethin' for you to wear, my beauty. That'll have to be whatsomever I can find, mind. There hen't been no young ladies in this here house, not for many a long year, that there hen't.'* Doesn't that do the job better, retaining a flavour of regional (Norfolk) speech while being easily comprehensible?

Historical dialogue has similar pitfalls: use archaic turns of phrase with great caution. Don't have everyone going around crying 'Forsooth, varlet!' and 'Gadzooks!' and 'Oddsbodikins!' Conversely, don't have your eighteenth-century maiden refuse a 'date', or speak about what a 'traumatic time' she's having – unless she's actually a time traveller from our century, of course!

Technical tips

Real conversations don't follow a pattern. People break off, interrupt each other, lose their tempers, change the subject . . . Some are voluble, some precise. Allude to these things as appropriate.

Try to avoid lengthy speeches. People seldom talk for long without a pause or an interruption. An exception is when a character has a story to tell, which in itself becomes narrative; break this up into normal paragraphs for ease of reading. (You would punctuate by leaving out the final quote mark in each paragraph, indicating that the speech is continuing in the next paragraph, which opens with another quote mark.)

You don't need to put in every bit of a conversation. You can say, *Mrs Fibbet went on and on about her Albert*, without recounting every word the talkative lady said. Reporting speech in this way we can ring the changes and also convey the gist of a conversation when finer details are unnecessary: *He asked me to go out with him, but I wasn't keen so I made an excuse* deals with what could be several lines of actual dialogue. On the other hand, if this relationship is a pivotal one in your story, recount the full conversation with all its nuances.

To study dialogue further, read good fiction and analyse how present-day authors are doing it. I suggest current authors rather than the old masters because today's readers are the ones you want to reach. Great though Charles Dickens may have been in his day, his methods are not necessarily what present publishers hope to see.

'The Christmas Present', our favourite story, has some examples of truly DIRE dialogue that will help to show what to avoid. (I've corrected basic faults of spelling and punctuation, to make it less messy.)

1. *'Well, Jim, what shall we do this evening?' enquired big Mick the Irishman. 'Sure and there are a couple of Proddies I should very much like to make sorry they were ever born, begorrah.'*

What a dreadful stereotype 'big Mick' is – even his name. Consider the speech itself. What does it do for the story? Very little. All it reveals is the author's ignorance and prejudice. The final *begorrah* is so clumsy it's laughable. Mrs D. would probably have every Scotsman saying 'hoots mon' and every Welshman uttering 'look you'. Characterization has to be far more subtle and intelligent than this.

What purpose does this speech have? Since Mick has nothing relevant to say, why let him speak? Why even give him a name? Why introduce him at all? He's not mentioned again, either earlier or later. So, having no role to play, he's dispensable. Thank goodness. Goodbye, Mick.

2. *'No, that's boring stuff,' replied Jim ironically. 'I vote we have a burn-up down the shopping precinct and see what's happening down there. There are a few old ladies we could mug and if not we can smash a shop window or two. It will be super fun.'*

More horrors here. What's ironical about Jim's speech? Nothing. Do today's bikers call it a 'burn-up'? Would even the awful Jim be so blatant about mugging old ladies and smashing shop windows, and is he really the type to use an expression like 'super fun'? None of it's in character, is it?

3. *'Oh, James,' ejaculated pretty Fiona, who he had on his rear seat. 'I would so love to have a necklace like that, only Ma hasn't got two halfpennies to rub together since our Dad run off with his fancy woman.'*

Where did Fiona suddenly appear from? She hasn't been mentioned before, but we're now told he 'had her on his rear seat' (those who can see the *double entendre* there, explain it to the rest, please. Quietly). Why use an ugly word like 'ejaculated' when plain English will do just as well — 'she said', 'she cried', 'she exclaimed'? And why does the last part of the speech go all pseudo-working class? I suspect Mrs D. has attempted a bit of characterization. But it hasn't worked, in any way, has it?

——————— o ———————

There follows a selection of different ways with dialogue. How would you edit them, if at all?

Recognizing the writing, I quickly tore open the envelope.
'Is it from him?' asked my wife hopefully.
'Yes, love, it is,' I said, returning to the lounge.
1 *'Read it to me, please,' she insisted gently.*
Sitting down beside her, I removed the letter from its envelope.
2 *'What are you doing?' demanded my wife. 'Read the letter.'*
'There's a photograph with it,' I told her.
3 *'A photograph?' she repeated excitedly. 'Is it of him?'*
4 *'Yes, my love,' I said. 'It is.'*
'Well, how does he look, what does he say? Oh, do hurry up.'
'I'm sorry, dear. Shall I read the letter first, then?'
'No, tell me about his picture. Does it show a girl with him?'
'No, love, there's no girl with him.'
'Oh.'
'Perhaps there was a girl,' I suggested. 'And she was the one taking the picture.'
5 *My wife smiled. 'I do hope you're right, dear.'*
'I'm sure I am. Now, would you like me to read the letter?'
'Not yet. I'd like you to describe his picture to me first.'

Comments: This author's work is spare, filled with feeling, and very short; he came to class to learn how to expand his ideas

– and how to write narrative, which, he said, he found almost impossible to do. Most beginners find the *dialogue* harder!

The whole piece (of which I've quoted about a third) runs to roughly 500 words, which is enough for the simple idea at its core – the woman's frustration with her blindness: her son is far away and she can't read his letter or even see his picture. At the end, she asks to hold the picture, and tears run down her face. Although it has nice feeling, it's too brief to be a story, as such, but as an exercise in natural dialogue it's good: we can deduce a lot about these two simply from what they say, can't we?

Even so, the extract I've quoted could be edited a little. In the lines marked 1–4, the narrative phrases could all be cut. In 1 the word *insisted* seems wrong, because she hasn't asked him to read the letter before, and the adverb *gently* is implied in the *please*: I would cut this phrase altogether, leaving just the dialogue. Similarly with 3. We know she's repeating, and it's clear she's excited, so that phrase too can be deleted. In 2 I'd prefer *she demanded* because we know she's his wife and there are only the two of them there, so 'she' can only mean the woman. 4: Again, since there are only the two of them, obviously they speak alternately, so the *I said* is expendable. 5: *wife* repeated again; a narrative phrase might do well here, e.g. *She seemed pleased by that idea.* What would *you* suggest?

The shorter and sparer the piece, the more careful you must be to have every single word right.

―――――   o   ―――――

Extract from a novel-in-progress:

The light from Bernard's porch starkly exposed the damage to the Jaguar's bumper.

'Driving too fast again, I see.' Bernard patted the wing above the dented metal. 'That'll cost a few bob.'

Alex pulled his holdall from the boot, deciding not to argue the point about his driving, even though Bernard was probably right. He pushed the lid down, then walked with Bernard along the drive towards the front of the house.

'On my way back this afternoon, I saw one of our lorries going down the M11. Couldn't see who was driving.'

'Think that might have been Harry – on the pumpkin run.'

'Pardon?'

'Hallowe'en, remember?' Bernard laughed. 'Those orange round things.'

'OK. OK. I know.' He spoke lightly, yet inwardly he was dismayed, discovering he had not noticed another year rapidly drawing to an end.

Comments: See how this establishes time of day, season of year, the relationship between the men and Alex's mood of distraction. Notice that the author hasn't used 'said' or its synonyms at all; instead, the dialogue is interspersed with pieces of narrative which further the action. However, it could be sharpened, clarified and pruned of cliché. Can you see where? How would you do that? Think about it, then turn to the end of the chapter for one way of editing it.

———— o ————

Next we meet Evie and her younger brother, Tim. She's driving him home from band practice:

'I played my solo tonight,' he informed me. 'Old Davo was gobsmacked. I was the business. Absolutely brill.'

'Modest, too,' I observed, but the irony went unnoticed.

'Even the wild man from Borneo says I've improved out of sight.

Not that he's any judge. Just because he can vamp a tune from a piano—'

'Shall we leave Geoff Wildman out of this?'

'Suits me. I can't think what you see in the pompous git, anyway.'

He had a lovely way with words.

Tim was seventeen, going on six and a half. His colouring echoed mine – fair with green-hazel eyes, but in everything else we were opposites. The seven-year gap in our ages made that inevitable, I suppose. I sometimes thought that only his musical talent saved him from being a total delinquent, but he had some endearing qualities and I was fond of the brat, even if he did have a habit of despising any man he considered to be a contender for my affections. Such as Geoff Wildman.

Comments: This passage sets the relationship between brother and sister (from her VP), sketches in a brief idea of what they look like, tells us how old they both are and introduces a third character (Geoff Wildman). Narrative tone of voice is light and dry, words like *brat* thrown in to echo Evie's feelings for her brother.

Another point for discussion – the use of slang, such as *gobsmacked* and *brill* could date this piece, unless it's intended to be firmly set in the 1980s (or thereabouts). If you want to keep a story feeling more up-to-date for longer, avoid extremes of current slang.

———— o ————

To set the next scene: it's night time, early 1940s. Choirboy David is outside the church, waiting for his friend Eric to arrive, when a bomb drops on the village . . .

The noise of the explosion terrified me for a moment. But I crept out of the porch to see a cloud of smoke hanging over the village as the sound of the fire engine followed the explosion.

'Hi,' I said as I first heard and then saw Eric in the moonlight. 'Did you hear that one?' I asked.

Eric said nothing as he stood in the shadow of the hedge. I could hardly see his face as he stooped and put a shoe box at my feet and turned and disappeared at unusual speed down the drive.

'What about . . .' But he had gone.

Old Baldy Pigeon said I would have to sing the carol as a solo instead of a duet. He had no time for anyone not sending their apologies. Eric would be for it after Christmas!

I felt a bit smug as I walked home. I knew I had sung the solo well and, although Eric was my best mate, I felt a bit superior at the thought of upstaging him on Christmas Day.

'Mum!' I shouted as I rushed in the front door. 'I'm to sing a solo as Eric couldn't stay for the practice. Oh! and he gave me this.' I held out the shoebox.

'I know,' she said, frowning.

'What?'

'I know Eric didn't go to church tonight.'

'But he did come, Mum. He gave me this box and went back home again.'

She knelt down and put her arms round me. 'I'm sorry, love, but I think you must have imagined it. That doodle-bug tonight dropped on Eric's house. I'm afraid that he and his family are all lost.'

Comments: In a short story, every word must count, but this author goes to the other extreme: he *leaves out* too much, hurrying through his story at such speed that he robs it of much of its emotional and dramatic impact. The gaps need filling if this is to become a satisfying, rounded story.

At the same time, a few redundant words and phrases ought to be cut: *I felt a bit smug . . . I felt a bit superior . . .* (repetition), and here and there the wording is awkward: *as I first heard and then saw Eric . . .* When the boy goes home, the dialogue could be extended a little to make it more convincing.

After much discussion, and several rewrites, this edited version emerged:

I wasn't scared, we were used to bombs by then, but the sudden explosion and blast sent me reeling into the porch and made my heart beat a little faster. A cloud of smoke and flames climbed into the night sky from the village below.

As a fire engine clanged its way through the darkness, I saw, with relief, the hunched figure of Eric as he rolled, hands in pockets, up the path towards me. Even in the darkness he was managing to kick a stone ahead of himself.

'Hi.'

'Hi,' I said and, in the same breath, 'Did you see that doodlebug? It must have come down near your street.'

'It did. Look, Dave, can you tell old Baldy I shan't be able to sing the carol tonight, or on Christmas Day?'

'Well, I'm not doing a solo! Why can't you come?'

'I . . . I just can't. I've got to go.'

As he turned to leave, he thrust something into my hands, muttering, 'That's because you're my best mate, and you haven't got a dad to give you presents.'

I was puzzled by Eric and the way he acted. As I watched him scurry away into the darkness, I thought how odd it was that he hadn't smiled once, when usually he had a permanent grin curling round his face.

I was wondering if I dared go into the church alone when old Baldy appeared and stalked past me into the musty building. I followed, trying to explain about Eric, but he only grunted, 'You'll have to sing it on your own, then.'

After practice, I felt a bit smug as I rushed off to tell Mum that I would be singing a solo on Christmas morning. But as I turned the corner of our street I saw Mum hurrying towards me.

'Hello, Mum.' I kissed her. 'What's the matter? You've never met me from church before.'

'No, dear.'

I sensed that something was wrong as she put her arm round me and walked me home in silence. Once inside the house, with the door shut, we were able to put the light on, and at once I could see that Mum was upset.

'David . . .' she said solemnly. 'A flying bomb has dropped on Elder Close.'

'I know! It must have been close to Eric's house.'

'I'm afraid it was on Eric's house,' she said even more gravely, 'and . . . and . . .'

'At least Eric is OK,' I blurted out as she struggled to finish her sentence.

'No, dear. No. I'm afraid . . . I'm afraid poor Eric was killed. He was in the house when the bomb . . .'

I didn't hear the rest. My mind was in turmoil. He couldn't have been hurt as I had spoken to him . . . I rushed to my room and slammed the door.

Although this is now considerably longer than the original, I think you'll agree that it's a more pleasing piece of writing. I'd have liked a line or two about David's feelings during choir practice — to prolong the tension before we have the explanation — and if it were my story I'd make a few more small changes to the wording. But it's not my story, so I'll leave it for you to decide whether it needs any more editing. What would *you* advise?

(NB We shall be looking at the ending of this particular story, along with others, in the chapter on — you've guessed it — 'Endings'.)

*

Did you note how these authors handled different VPs and 'tones of narrative voice'? Go back and look again at that aspect.

———————— o ————————

Of the above examples, only the first has more than two people talking; so we'll look at one final extract which introduces several characters, in early Victorian times. It comes from my novel *Sandringham Rose*.

Lady Mary's reverie was invaded by the arrival of her two oldest grandsons, Jonathan and Seward, both in their thirties, the older one thin and restless, the other growing broader with every year. Jonathan stalked the carpet with long-legged, jerky strides, reminding his grandmother of a mantis, while Seward took up his favourite position by the hearth, back to the fire, glass in one hand. A gold watch chain gleamed across the black silk waistcoat that swathed his paunch.

It amused Lady Mary that her grandchildren resembled the cattle of Pharaoh's dream — some lean kine and some fat kine. The lean ones took after their late father, her son, James; the fat ones were more like their mother.

Anne Hamilton came in behind her sons, skirts swaying, corsets struggling to contain her ample waist. Her grey hair was tortured into fashionable ringlets dangling either side of a face moulded into lines of disapproval by years of practice.

'We thought we'd find you here,' she said, settling in the middle of a settee. 'Mama, we want to talk to you. About Will.'

Lady Mary took a sip of port and carefully replaced the glass on the table beside her. She dabbed a lace handkerchief to her lips. 'What about Will?'

'My reply exactly!' Seward exclaimed. 'I knew you'd understand,

Grandmama. Grief takes people in different ways. He'll come to his senses. But he needs time.'

'Time to make a complete fool of himself,' Jonathan snorted. 'I hardly care to imagine what everyone must be saying after today's performance. I agree it's hard to lose a wife, but does one have to lose one's head as well?'

Seward slanted him a gleaming look. 'Perhaps one does. How would you know? Will isn't like the rest of us. Never has been, never will be. A changeling, I shouldn't wonder.'

His mother quelled him with a glance, her face pinched. 'I find your humour in very poor taste, Seward.'

'You should know by now, Mama,' Jonathan said, 'that to include Seward in a discussion of any gravity is like asking a crow to sing like a nightingale. The question is, what are we, as his family — as Hamiltons — to do about this?'

Seward threw out his hands. 'Why should we do anything? Will's a grown man. Let him plan his own life.'

'But a tenant farmer!' Anne Hamilton exclaimed. 'It's not the thing. It's really not.'

Lady Mary, sitting erect in her high-backed chair with one hand resting on her cane, said gruffly, 'On this occasion I agree with Seward. The best action is no action. Stand neutral. That's my advice.'

Jonathan grimaced. 'You always were too lenient with Will, Grandmama.'

Ignoring that, for she had heard the charge many times and was bored with it — especially since it was true — she looked at her daughter-in-law. 'And the children? What does he propose to do with the children?'

This is part of the introductory chapter, which establishes the background for Rose Hamilton's story. The purpose of this scene is to show the kind of family she has to contend with.

Just before this extract begins, we have seen Lady Mary alone, her physical appearance, her surroundings and her thoughts. Then comes this sketch of two of her grandsons, and their mother, still from Lady Mary's VP. It establishes exact relationships, so the reader knows clearly who these people are. Then they begin to speak and reveal their different characters: Jonathan is pompous, concerned with appearances, speaks in correct sentences; Seward is more liberal, even flippant, with a more staccato rhythm to his speech. What would you say are the main traits of the two women as shown here? Are they distinct, separate beings?

Technical points to notice: With four people on stage, sign-posts to who's speaking are more frequent, not always verbs of saying – small pieces of narrative do the job in places. Speech verbs are fairly basic, unadorned by adverbs. Is this enough? Does the dialogue itself tell you *how* these sentences were spoken?

Since we entered on Lady Mary's VP, we remain in her perceptions, privy to no thoughts but hers. But the VP takes a long view, it's not closely inside the old lady's head reacting to every nuance. It doesn't need to be: none of these characters is to play a major part in the drama that follows. This scene's *only* function is to sketch an overall picture of the kind of people the Hamilton family are.

Does it do that? You're the reader, only you can judge.

———— o ————

RECAP

- Dialogue has many functions, but it should always **move the story along**.
- Be frugal with verbs of speech; use them as signposts.
- Don't use unnecessary adverbs: let the context, and the words spoken, do the work instead.
- Vary the pattern on the page with pieces of narrative.
- Make use of reported speech where appropriate.
- Avoid stereotypes of both speech and character.
- Keep dialogue true to character.
- Keep dialect to a flavouring minimum.

Two Exercises:
Write a short duologue (two people only), using as few pieces of narrative as possible. Let the spoken words tell the story, as in the introduction to this chapter.
AND
Put the following into direct speech:
1. The driver addressed me abruptly, asking if I was from Lynn.
2. She enquired, rather sarcastically, if he was aware how much phone calls cost these days.
3. Max queried the meaning of the word 'scatty'.
4. As he opened the car door, he told her to move over.
5. Roughly, Carl said she should stop being so stupid.

Think about the next two examples – if asked to 'report' the first and turn the second into direct speech, how would you go about it? Do you think your versions are an improvement, or are they better left as they are?

6. 'So he says,' Mrs Turnip gossiped, '"Annie wouldn't have done that," he says. So I says, "Blast, and she would!" And so she would!'
7. He insisted on putting the car into the barn for me, so I got out and directed him into the narrow space.

(Suggested answers are on page 207–8)

Edited piece from page 125:

The light from the porch exposed the damage to the Jaguar's bumper.

'Driving too fast again, I see.' Bernard patted the wing above the dented metal. 'That'll cost a few bob.'

Alex pulled his holdall from the boot, deciding not to argue. His friend was probably right about his driving. He followed Bernard to the front door, saying, 'On my way back this afternoon I saw one of our lorries going down the M11. Couldn't see who was driving.'

'Probably Harry – on the pumpkin run.'

'Pardon?'

'Those orange round things?' Bernard laughed. 'Hallowe'en, remember?'

'OK. OK. I know.' Despite the lightness of his tone, he was dismayed to realize how quickly the year was passing.

8 · Description
– Painting Pictures with Words

On looking through my volunteers' work for examples for this chapter, I was interested to discover few passages of actual description. Often, writers had used familiar, modern-day settings which allowed them to escape by merely saying *the office* or *the sitting room of the bungalow* and letting the reader do the rest of the work. But even in the odd historical story or unusual location not many had tried to create vivid pictures for their readers. Presumably, since these were only class exercises, the writers hadn't done much in the way of research. Perhaps, also, they avoided evocation for fear of its supposed problems.

Descriptive writing seems to have a reputation for being difficult, but it's no more so than writing dialogue, portraying character or creating a good plot. Without it, your work is only half done. I feel that good descriptive writing is the glue that holds the rest together.

Sparkling, buzzing, cool, pungent, salty – and mobile

Good evocative writing does more than paint pictures: it brings in all *six* senses – not only the way things look but how they sound, what it feels like to touch them, what scents (or stenches) fill the air, how taste buds react, and what *feelings* are evoked – not all at the same time, but added here and there to deepen the reader's experience. If you remember all the senses, you can add extra touches of reality to your writing. So **be observant**. Take note of what sounds, scents, sensations you experience in different situations.

But try to avoid creating long screeds of description (however well-written), where nothing else happens. The golden rule is, **don't let it hold up the story**. There may be exceptions to this rule (there always are) but *most of the time* you DON'T pause to tell your reader all about the scenery and then let the characters make their next move; you intersperse your description with action and dialogue, mixing it all together so that it blends into a pleasing whole that carries the reader along with it. In other words, you create *moving* pictures.

To demonstrate, here's another piece from *The Clouded Land*, my World War One novel.

Kate and her escort have just arrived in Norfolk, by rail, both weary and having just had words:

In the station yard, a horse and cart waited for us.

'They din't say nothin' about passengers,' the driver complained. 'That old cart en't very comfortable for a lady.'

'Well, it'll have to do,' said my escort.

However, just as the man was loading the last trunk, a car roared into the yard and my uncle, Frank Rhys-Thomas, leapt out of it.

'Kate!' he cried, enveloping me in a bear hug before holding me at arm's length to look at me critically. 'You look terrible,' he informed me bluntly. 'What on earth have they done to you, girl?'

'Oh . . . Uncle Frank, I'm so glad to see you!' Feeling like a lost child suddenly finding a friend, I threw my arms around him.

(Here, some necessary story-developing dialogue ensues. The escort is left behind as Kate and her uncle set off for home.) Then:

Midway to the village, he turned on to a track. As we climbed the hill I could see the sea.

'Christ!' said my uncle.

A man had stepped out from the hedge ahead. He held a shotgun levelled at our windscreen.

I've included the last segment because it introduces another character, so we've met three people new to the story: the driver of the cart, Uncle Frank, and the man with the shotgun. Each has varying importance in the story to come. Kate and her escort have been described in earlier scenes. But how clearly could you picture the new characters, or the scene through which they moved? Probably not clearly at all, because I've *removed most of the description*.

You may have filled in some gaps from your own imagination, but I doubt that the resulting picture was what I *intended* you to see. Let's find out. Here's the scene as *I* visualize it:

In the station yard, a horse and cart waited for us. The driver seemed nervous, anxious to be on his way before the storm broke.

'They din't say nothin' about passengers,' he complained. 'That old cart en't very comfortable for a lady.'

'Well, it'll have to do,' said my escort.

However, just as the man was loading the last trunk, a large open-topped motor car, magnificent with silver paintwork and silver-plate fittings under a film of dust, roared into the yard. Trailing a choking cloud of yet more dust, it slewed round to halt beside me amid a spattering of small stones. As the dust cleared, my uncle, Frank Rhys-Thomas, grinned up at me, doffing his battered Panama as he leapt out of the car. He reminded me of a grasshopper, long legs in ancient cricket trousers worn with a loose, paint-stained shirt.

'Kate!' he cried, enveloping me in a bear hug before holding me at arms' length to look at me critically. He was in his early thirties,

an attractive though not handsome man. In a tanned face framed by a tangled mane of dark-gold waves so long they fell over his shapeless collar, slate-blue eyes had narrowed with concern. 'You look terrible,' he informed me bluntly. 'What on earth have they done to you, girl?'

'Oh . . . Uncle Frank, I'm so glad to see you!' Feeling like a lost child suddenly finding a friend, I threw my arms around him, leaning my cheek to his strong shoulder. He smelled of linseed, and musk, and fresh sea air.

He swept open the low door of the tourer and gestured me inside. The car was amply big enough for four or five people, but the wide back seat was littered with painting paraphernalia – canvases and paints, brushes, rags, an easel thrown in at an ungainly angle, the whole roughly covered by a rumpled linen jacket.

.   .   .

Midway to the village, he turned on to a rutted farm track, iron-hard after weeks of drought. Ahead of us lay the hill, wooded and dark under lowering clouds, branches swept by the strengthening wind. The track forked, the left hand branch leading past a pond and huge barns to an old farmhouse with low thatched roof and many chimneys, set back among sheltering trees. We took the right fork, between tall thorn hedges, bucketing over ridges that shook the car and rattled my teeth. A plume of dust rose behind us, and huge drops of rain spat down, harbingers of the storm. The clouds had all but covered the sky, turning the day to dusk. As we climbed the hill I could see the surface of the sea churned into choppy waves, the far shore obscured behind a mist of rain.

'Christ!' said my uncle.

A man had stepped out from the hedge ahead, a bulky, bristle-chinned figure in shapeless hat and weatherproof cape, corduroys gartered by string at his knees. He held a shotgun levelled at our windscreen.

Though this is now considerably lengthened, it gives a much clearer picture of the scene as I *wanted* you to see it, *for the purposes of my story*. See how the senses have been included – sights, sounds, sensation, smell ... There's dust flying, a storm about to break, Kate's teeth rattling over the bumps, the smell of linseed ... The car is shown in detail for three good fictional reasons: it helps to emphasize the period; it gives us an insight into Frank's character; and, in this book, the car itself plays a part in the plot, so it must impinge itself on the reader's mind. Similarly with the setting: the farm in its valley under the hill, even the short-cut track across the farmer's land, have vital roles to play in what follows, which is why they, too, are described in detail.

You can now see how the three new characters are painted with different emphasis – the cart driver remains a vague figure because he's a bit player, not important to the plot. Uncle Frank is presented in detail – he's to be one of the major protagonists. And the man with the shotgun is, for now, briefly but memorably (I hope) sketched in; he has to establish himself in the reader's mind, because he too is going to be a major figure in the plot: this is amplified by the subsequent conversation between Kate and her uncle – naturally they *discuss* this alarming incident.

So ... the lesson is that you carefully choose how much description to give to which bit of the scene, **depending on its importance to the plot**. And, all the time, mingled with the description, the characters are moving, speaking and reacting to each other, to the scene, and to the objects around them.

Our example of how-not-to, the story by Cassandrina Dustworthy, begins with a detailed description of her main character. In the light of what we've been discussing, what do you think of her descriptive efforts now?

Emily Cartwright was a widow in her late fifties. Emily had grey hair and blue eyes and stood about five foot three inches tall. Emily wore her hair in little curls along her forehead, and her features were sharp, an aquiline nose with high cheekbones and thin lips. But despite her appearance Emily was a kindly, unassuming sort of person, who always kept her home neat and tidy.

Apart from the fact that most of this is irrelevant to the story, it's very badly written. Sentences are too uniform; detail is fussy and, as it turns out, inaccurate – when we read the rest of the story, Emily doesn't come over as kindly and unassuming, does she? Rather, she reveals herself as a narrow-minded bigot (at least, the *author* reveals *herself* thus; she has not got inside Emily's head at all). Worst of all, the paragraph is static – nothing is happening.

If Mrs D. really felt that we had to know what Emily looked like, she ought to have written it more entertainingly, blending it with action. Say: *Emily Cartwright sank into a chair, thankful for a few minutes' peace. She wore her grey hair sculpted into curls along her brow, a frizzy pelmet for a bony face with thin lips. Since her husband died, she had lived alone . . .* At least Emily is now *doing* something, if only sitting in a chair, and she's *feeling* something – she's *thankful*. She's becoming a character, not just a two-dimensional picture. Her stature is not significant to the story, nor her exact age: grey hair gives us a clue that she's not young, and the rest of the story will confirm her approximate vintage.

Later, the author treats us to a further passage of description: *. . . a particularly well-dressed window of a large emporium. It was brightly lit and had a magnificent display of gifts all wonderfully arranged at various heights on fat pedestals all draped with thick black velvet to set off the colourful goods and tempt the eager shopper into parting with there hard-earned cash. There were* *lacquered fans of exquisite design, terra-cotta pots with silk flowers arranged in them very tastefully indeed, silk scarves of every hue under the sun, and a dazzling host of other most delightful and attractive goods ideal for Christmas presents for close friends and family. They were all cleverly set out with glittering tinsel and shiny baubles in a masterful display of the window-dresser's art.*

James slammed on his brakes and reversed his machine, gazing with greedy eyes at a particularly beautiful brooch . . .

Here's more bad writing: it completely holds up the action (in a story of this brevity, you have no time for long pauses of this kind) and little of it is relevant – *the brightly lit window of a department store, full of Christmas gifts* would have been enough since all it serves to do in the story is provide a venue for the robbery.

However, setting aside those criticisms, look at it purely as a piece of writing. What do you think of it?

For me, it's full of vagaries and woolly waffle, larded with too many adjectives; every noun and verb seems to have at least one and sometimes several 'describing words'. The paragraph does build a picture, but what a waste of waffle goes with it: *particularly well-dressed . . . magnificent display . . . wonderfully arranged . . . exquisite design . . . a host of other most delightful and attractive goods . . . very tastefully indeed . . .*This is verbal diarrhoea, superlatives that mean nothing, vague phrases that, far from being descriptive, add not a touch of concrete information. Watch out for the redundant word 'very' – use it only where absolutely necessary, and if you find yourself writing the Blytonesque 'very . . . indeed', then stay behind after class and write out lists of vibrant, vital verbs that do away with such padding and help your prose to sparkle. One of your characters may get away with this floppy English, but please don't do it in your narrative.

As for viewpoint, well, this is certainly not seen from James's

VP, is it? He wouldn't get lyrical over a shop window, or pontificate about eager shoppers parting with hard-earned cash. No, the VP is solely the author's. Was she a window-dresser in some other existence?

We won't even bother to mention her habit of starting so many sentences in flat, boring fashion: *It was . . .*; *There were . . .* (See section on style, page 179.) So much for Mrs D.

———— o ————

The following comes from the first draft of a novel. Bearing in mind that, in a book, you *can* take time to describe more fully, would you advise the author to edit this piece and, if so, how?

The first person narrator is arriving in a taxi:

Ahead of us now, the defensive mounds around the castle came into sight. Erected in the twelfth century, the earth banks remained as evidence of the military grandeur which had once existed there. Inside the circular defences, a park dotted with trees now surrounded the ruined remains of the castle itself, part of a wall and one turret, and the old house stood to one side. It had once been a manor, then a farmhouse, added to and revamped over the centuries until it stood as a monument to several different styles of architecture, with tall Georgian chimneys rising above leaded windows. When John Westland, aunt Chloe's late husband, had bought the place, he had had the interior redesigned and he had sold off most of the land to neighbouring farmers, so that now the house was simply a country residence, quietly sumptuous and with a unique charm.

As I paid the taxi driver, the main door of the house opened and Aunt Chloe rushed out to greet me with hugs and kisses. She was a small lady, her hair cut short and held back with a plastic Alice band, her dumpy figure draped in a shapeless cotton dress, and flat sandals on her bare feet. No one seeing her would have guessed she was a wealthy widow; she looked more like a penniless spinster. But Aunt Chloe didn't care what people thought. She was eccentric in that she dressed and behaved entirely to please herself.

After three lines of commonplace 'greeting' dialogue, aunt and niece go into the house, where we're given seven more lines of description of the niece's bedroom, followed by an account of the aunt's history.

I confess — this is one of *my* early efforts, never finished. I found it among piles of other discards, in the attic. Before I tell you what I now consider is wrong with it, what do *you* think?

Comments: In my opinion, the piece says both too much and too little: the words are there but they don't evoke a clear picture — not for me, and I dreamed up this darn place! The only solid description in the first paragraph tells of defensive earth banks, a park dotted with trees, a ruined castle (wall and turret), and a house with tall Georgian chimneys and leaded windows. I get no impression of distances or size, no colour (is the house stone or brick?), no real picture of the place at all. It *stood to one side*, but which side, and how far away? It was *a monument to different styles of architecture . . . a country residence, quietly sumptuous and with a unique charm* — meaningless verbiage, as bad as Mrs Dustworthy's.

Then the aunt: *She was . . .* that uninspired opening again, used twice in this paragraph. The last two and a half sentences, from *widow*, ought to be cut. Chloe should reveal *herself* to the reader, by word and deed.

Did you notice, also, that the piece is purely visual? It involves none of the senses except sight, and it remains a static, black and white, and rather blurred image.

Finally, what's missing is any sense of continuing story: no tension, no conflict, no hooks or telegraphs to make the reader want to read on to find out what happens. As I can see now, what I did was halt the story while I got the dreaded description over. Knowing myself not best at that area of writing, I compounded the error by doing it in chunks, sighing with relief, then getting on with the action and the dialogue, which I did enjoy.

Nowadays, I would probably try to find some real house that fitted my idea, or imagine a composite of real places I had seen. It's much easier to describe something vividly if you yourself have a clear picture of it, so use any tricks or aids you can think of: studying pictures, reading travel books ... So long as you don't use another author's exact words, you can employ his experience to add to your own. (It's called research.) Best of all, *visit* the places you want to describe. Go out and use your eyes, your ears, your senses ...

That old adage, **Write about what you know**, is still good advice, though far from a hard and fast rule. Imagination does have a place. How else can you write about murder, or history, or other planets? I would change the advice to **Write about what you know; what you don't know, at present, go and find out!**

―――――― o ――――――

Rather than try to rewrite the above discard, let me show you a more recent extract which has a similar theme – a young woman arriving at a house. This, too, is a first, rough draft, another fragment of a book I abandoned, but I think it's an improvement on the one above.

This narrator is arriving on foot ...

Deserted as it seemed, the wood was far from silent. Rain dripped from the canopy of leaves, pattering into a lush undergrowth of bramble and bracken. Pigeons mourned not far away, and a family of pheasant ran jerkily across the muddy track. Nature herself seemed to be stirring, settling her gown of leaves and grasses and drinking in the rain.

And then, round a bend, I came in sight of what must be my destination. 'Primrose Farm' was a bit pretentious for it, but I'd known more fanciful names for even smaller places.

It looked long deserted – except, as I stopped, I fancied I heard the last chords of a piano piece, so someone was at home. Mrs Charteris was expecting me, anyway. Beyond a tangle of over-grown lilacs and buddleias whose flowers had turned to dried brown spikes, the thatched roof lifted, thin and grey with age, sagging a little. The windows were dull with months of dirt; the frames needed a coat of fresh paint; the lawn was a wild jungle of long grasses, sorrel and buttercups, and the flowerbeds were choked by chickweed. No one had worked in that garden for a long time, probably all summer.

Somehow the cottage didn't fit with the brisk, efficient voice that had spoken to me on the phone. I caught myself concocting theories to explain it, which, as James always said, was one of my problems – too much imagination.

As I laid my hand on the gate, a twig cracked loudly under my foot, causing a partridge to rise in a whirr of wings. In its wake, the silence seemed deeper, still underlined by that steady dripping, and by the stirrings that seemed evidence of continuing growth and decay.

Perhaps I was in a fanciful mood. The place seemed to be frozen in time, separated from the real world. Sleeping Beauty might lie here, hidden by her fairy godmothers, or was King Arthur slumbering, waiting for the call to rise at England's need, or the Earth Mother herself, held in thrall by enchantments while mankind, let

*loose like some manic child, pillaged and desecrated and
destroyed her? I found myself wanting to take a scythe to the wild
growth, a pair of secateurs to the overblown rosebushes, a chamois
leather to the windows, and a paintbrush to the door. I wanted to
wake the place, to rescue it from ruin.*

In fact, it was love at first sight.

This piece still needs a fair amount of work. That penultimate
paragraph gets *too* fanciful and purple-proseish, but it can be
cut. I also notice that in one place I've put *The windows were
. . . The lawn was . . . The flowerbeds were . . .* I'd try to change
at least two of those passive verbs to active ones, say: *Months
of dirt dulled the windows . . . Chickweed choked the lawn . . .*
(see Chapter Eleven).

But in general this piece is much more lively than the last.
More of the senses are involved; it includes a touch of mystery
and a hint of contention – the conflict elements that keep the
reader reading. Although it's told in a fairly light-hearted way,
there are hints of darker undertones. It's altogether deeper and
richer than the earlier example.

Do you agree, or would you argue?

——————— o ———————

In contrast, a true-life article begins:

*The droplets of water glistened like diamonds caught in the brilliant
Mediterranean sunshine as the dolphins gleefully leapt high out of
the water just ahead of the bows of the boat, forcing the helmsman
to throttle back the engines swiftly. Dippy had come in close from
nowhere. All the watchers on deck had been too entranced with
the coincidence of the emergence of the threatening black hull of
the French nuclear submarine a few hundred yards behind the*

catamaran, just as Mike, their host, had finished telling the group about the English vessel that had left the bay the weekend previously.

All the crew stood above the deck at presentation stations. There were no sailors on top of the boat today, only the French flag. The boat cut smoothly through the heavy swell . . .

This is another very rough draft, dashed off in a few minutes. Even so, it's more than a little confusing. We have a boat, a submarine, a catamaran, dolphins (one called Dippy?), a helmsman, Mike the host, watchers on the deck, crew standing *above the deck*, but *no sailors on top of the boat* . . . Which vessel is which, and who is where on which of them? It's a bit like a surrealist painting: all the pieces are there, but in no comprehensible order.

The first two sentences are too long, with too many different things happening all at once. They need breaking up into more easily digestible pieces, with clearer explanations of exactly what's happening. There's the same kind of flashback we've seen once or twice before: *had been entranced . . . had finished telling . . .* Taking this a step further back in time, into the pluperfect tense, distances us from the action. I feel that a moment earlier in the trip would make a better beginning, so that we can see it in sequence and share the building excitement as the watchers go out in search of dolphins . . .

How did it strike you?

One final piece exemplifies ways of combining evocation of time and place with continuation of plot and character development. Because this scene takes place in a real place (Hunstanton, Norfolk), at a defined time (Whit Monday) of a stated year (1890), considerable research has gone into it, to make the picture as accurate as possible:

The coachman had prepared the yellow phaeton for the journey, with its hood up to shelter Nanny and Bella while Jess and the picnic hamper rode in the smaller railed back seat behind the bulge of the great yellow hood. Not that Jess minded: the seat was high enough for her to see over most of the hedges, with wide views over rolling farmland down to the lines of white foam-horses dashing on the edge of the sea a mile away.

By mid-morning they were in New Hunstanton, along with several hundred other people coming in by road and rail, some on the new-fangled bicycles, which made Bella stare and point. The town green, set on a slope above the sea, was merry with stalls and sideshows. Jess kept her new straw boater well down, but no one took notice of the phaeton as it went clopping down the hill.

Soon they were queuing to pay their toll to the uniformed pier-master and mingling with the crowds along boards that stretched hundreds of feet into the Wash, protected by wrought iron railings. Jess had been to Hunstanton ten years before, on an outing with her family, but she hadn't been on the pier – Mother and Dad hadn't the money to pay for all the family to go, so they'd settled for the beach, which was free.

Nanny Fyncham planted herself and the picnic hamper on the first vacant bench, while Bella dragged Jess off to explore the pier. It was lined with seats, and refreshment kiosks with bunting fluttering in the mild sea breeze. They went to the very end, where steamers from Lynn dropped their passengers. Green waves were breaking against the iron piles below. One or two hardy souls came shivering out of bathing machines, stripped down to blue serge costumes as they ventured into the cold water. The sight made Jess shudder.

In this, we see the phaeton, and Jess content in her sub-servient position, with brief impressions of the countryside through which they're riding. Mingled with the description of the town, young Bella reacts to what she sees and we're reminded of Jess's fear of being seen by someone who knows her. She thinks of happier times in the past (she existed long before we met her; her family, fisherfolk of King's Lynn, would have visited Hunstanton on treat days). Then comes the pier (no longer there, but it existed, as described, in 1890).

Note that, although we view the scene from a distance, the thoughts we share remain Jess's; it's her VP, though we're seeing a full-length picture rather than an intimate close-up with a lot of introspection. The phrase *new-fangled bicycles* is, of course, Jess's way of thinking.

Only the tip . . .

When you're writing of places and times less familiar to your reader, you need to be even more careful to describe the scene, the clothes, the food and so forth fully and clearly. But do it judiciously. However much research you may have done, don't be tempted to put in every last bit of it simply to show off your erudition. Use only enough to paint the picture for your reader. Learn how to tell when you've over-written and CUT IT OUT. Or, as one famous teacher of creative writing (Sir Arthur Quiller-Couch) put it: 'Murder your darlings'. However much it hurts your writer's pride, carefully considered excision can only improve your writing. The unwritten part of your research will be in your mind, providing a solid basis to make the story authentic, but most of it remains hidden.

For an example of effective historical fiction, take a look at

Ellis Peters' Cadfael novels, which bring to vivid and colourful life the unusual setting of the first civil war in England, the Stephen/Matilda turmoil of the twelfth century AD.

RECAP

- Write about what you know; what you don't know, at present, find out!
- Be observant.
- Have the picture clear in your own mind.
- Include hints of as many senses as you can.
- Create moving pictures, not stills.
- Mix description with action and dialogue.
- Amount of description depends on demands of plot.
- **Don't let it hold up the story.**

Exercises:

1. Wherever you are as you read this, open your senses and find words to describe what you see, hear, touch, smell and taste, and what emotions you are currently experiencing.

2. Imagine yourself in a city centre, on top of a mountain, deep in a pine forest, lost in a desert, and diving in a lagoon. For each one of these, think what might excite each one of your five senses. Don't worry about being accurate at this stage, just *imagine*, vividly. Feel yourself there. (How would you go about checking the accuracy of your imaginings?)

3. Write a brief piece for at least one of the above venues, trying to find new ways of expressing your ideas. Avoid clichés and be sparing with adjectives, using only those that are *vital* to the piece.

9 · Structure and Plotting

Readers ask, 'Do you work in a flood of wild inspiration, or from a synopsis?' Answers vary as much as writers do, because method depends on what you're writing, and how your mind works. The first draft of a short story may be written at one sitting, or it may take painful weeks, even working with nothing but your imagination; the first draft of an article of the same length may require a good deal of research and planning. And any full-length book requires *some* preparatory work.

So, having looked at character drawing, dialogue and descriptive writing, let's take a look at the structure that lies underneath the words you're using.

Pattern under the prose

All prose has a pattern, which we can break down under general headings of Beginning, Middle and Ending. In Chapter Five we saw how vital it is to have a good beginning and we shall be discussing endings later; middle sections can be more fluid.

Articles are usually brief: you have a few hundred words in which to state your case, so use every word to effect. You may find it helpful to draft out a skeleton of facts, marshalling them in a clear, logical, understandable order. Get down to the subject immediately, don't waffle with introductory paragraphs which have no relevance to the main point; then introduce the rest of your material in considered sequence. End on a strong note, with a fact even more striking than the rest, perhaps a discovery you've made while researching, or with a punchy quote, or a reference back to the beginning.

The following two examples of articles take the same theme – lavender-growing in Norfolk.

The first begins: *People, one gathers, have been crowding to Hunstanton to see the lavender fields . . .* This introduces the subject well enough, but why does the writer say *one gathers* as if there's some doubt about the statement's veracity? That small phrase spoils his opening. A brief one hundred and fifty words later, he ends, *Yet years ago it was a different story. Lavender plants in Britain generally got badly out of condition through disease, and it seemed that English lavender perfume had become a thing of the past. This is all changed now.* This ending is equally weak, a let-down rather than a satisfying, well-rounded punch. Can you see that?

The second sample, headlined 'Dollars in Lavender', starts: *Rose Lee bent her back and grasped fifty mauve spears with one brown hand. In the other hand she held a small knife. 'Off with you,' she said, and the spears fell before the tiny blade.* This graphic opening uses fiction techniques to grab the reader's attention. The article goes on to describe the work of the lavender harvest and the process of distilling the oil, which will go mostly to America to earn dollars. It introduces the horticulturist who began it all, recounts how he developed the business and concludes with a nice quote that reveals his enthusiasm for the job as he watches his workers bend to their task in the field. The author ends: *Clearly, to Mr Chilvers, lavender means a good deal more than £sd – or dollars.* So the end loops back to the beginning, back to the title.

In a **non-fiction book** you might start with a list of chapter headings, or break it into sections, depending what suits your material best. A travel book might be divided into areas of a country, each section prefaced by a map of the area under discussion; it doesn't dot about, jumping from place to place illogically. See how I've arranged this book – the basic structure was there in my mind before I began: I swapped segments around slightly as I worked, until they found what seemed to be their best order; then my kindly copy-editor suggested a few further changes which made sense and helped the logical flow of the book (another mind is a great help when you yourself are so close to the work you can't see the forest for the oaks that are in the way).

If in doubt on how to tackle your non-fiction book, look in the library and see how other authors have dealt with a similar problem.

Short stories also need coherent shape, a strong beginning and a snappy ending. Their shape, you'll recall, is a climbing slope of tension culminating in a single peak of resolution, with a swift end-tying finish. Many stories have as their basis a character in need of something, something out of balance in his life, something that needs putting right before he can be happy again.

We could group story plots into three main types: **dispute**, **choice** and **realization**.

Dispute involves some kind of overt conflict, where the character has a goal to reach but someone else stands in opposition. The plot tells of the struggle, leading up to a major confrontation where (usually) the main character succeeds in his quest.

Choice is where the character has some need to fulfil, or a problem that has to be solved, but she must find the right way of doing it. Here, too, another person may stand against her, or it may be simply events, or fate, or her own nature she's struggling with. We see her striving, floundering, until some decisive moment when she's forced to make that final telling choice.

In **realization**, the character's main adversary is himself – he has some fatal flaw to overcome before he can win through or 'come to realize' his solution; this is often a quiet, gentle sort of story. Mrs Dustworthy tried to do it in 'The Christmas Present' but she didn't bring it off, as you'll recall. In another, very simple little story, a tired and frustrated young mother felt that her husband didn't love her any more: perhaps she should leave him. But she heard her little daughter speak of 'mummyandaddy' as if they were one being, and that persuaded her that she had something worth fighting for.

We've mentioned the need to keep a **full-length novel**'s plot rising towards the climax, the final revelation, the moment when everything is resolved. You aim to do this in a series of peaks and dips, building tension, then releasing it a little only to let it build even more. In my early work, I tended to introduce conflicts singly, resolving each one before starting the next. This left my work full of flat areas devoid of the continuing tension which acts as a barbed lure, keeping the reader hooked. One way to ensure continuing tension is always to have several on-going conflicts to work with; as you ease pressure on one, you start to build it up with another. Ideally, you should use all three types of plot – dispute, choice and realization – with as many variations as you can handle effectively.

For an example of weak structure, take a fresh look at Charles Dickens's classic *Great Expectations*. Dickens was ham-strung because he wrote for a monthly newspaper; being forced to finish each part to meet a deadline, he had no chance to go back and rework his plots: the first chapters were published before he'd written the last few. The wonder is he managed to write such marvellous stories under such conditions. *Great Expectations* has a rattling good start with the boy Pip, old Miss Havisham in her mouldering house, the proud Estella, the kindly Gargerys, and the terrifying Magwitch, but later the story loses its way and Dickens has to search for enough material to fill out the required episodes before he reaches his rather flat, contrived and unsatisfying conclusion. If he were to return and try a rewrite, he might want to make some changes. Look at this book again (the book, not one of the film versions) and see if you agree that its overall shape could be better.

For an example of rising peaks and dips, think of a mystery story, taking as its main plot thread the solving of a murder, the victims being the hero's wife and child. The man sets out to uncover the killer and have revenge. Along the way, he encounters friends and enemies, including a girl to whom he's attracted. False clues lead him into dangers; he believes he has the villain identified; some friends reveal themselves as enemies; he has doubts about the girl's trustworthiness; halfway through the book the supposed villain turns up dead, so there must be an even bigger baddie somewhere, but who is it? Now our hero doesn't know who to trust. The girl disappears and he gets deeper into trouble finding her, still not knowing whether she's deceiving him or not. All the time he's getting closer to unmasking the murderer . . . Can you see how this plot builds, conflict on conflict, towards the denouement where all questions will be answered? The identity of the villain; which person is trustworthy and which not; whether he cares for the girl, and she him . . . The author has to keep the strands tightly in his grip, not losing sight of any of them. His reader will expect *all* the loose ends to be tied up, in a logical and satisfactory manner, before the last full stop is printed.

The plot thickens

When creating a convoluted detective story, you may need to work to a **tightly plotted synopsis**, worked out chapter by chapter, in order to plant your clues and red herrings in the right places. The trap here is that, in order to follow your plan, your characters could become little more than cardboard cut-outs, existing solely for the sake of the plot, rather than the plot evolving from what your people do and how they think and feel. Be aware of that possible hazard, and read detective novels analytically, to see how their writers avoid it (or not).

The **'organic' method of plotting**, which suits me and the kind of books I write, is rather like going on a journey. You know where you're starting from; you know which leading players are going along (minor ones may join the party late, or take their leave en route); and you know, roughly, where your destination lies. But the route the characters take is up to them; they decide its exact course as they come to life and begin to relate to each other, sometimes in ways you, their creator, failed to predict (all creators/gods/parents have this problem). *Your* function is to control the pace of the journey, to bear in mind the demands of the novel's internal rhythm, driving at breakneck speed through action scenes, striding over puddles of passing time and necessary information, and on occasion pausing by the roadside to watch the sun rise in misty splendour. (If I take this analogy much further I shall risk careering over the cliff of verbosity into the morass of purple prose, but perhaps you get the idea.)

I, personally, have difficulty working to a detailed synopsis. Knowing exactly what's going to happen takes out most of the excitement for me. At times, when offering a book proposal to a publisher, I've had to provide a synopsis of some kind, but when I come to write the book I always have to change some details — my characters oblige me to do so; they take over and refuse to behave as I'd planned. (My publishers, I may say, have never objected to these necessary changes: if the book works, they're happy.) For instance, in chapter ten, a synopsis might call for my hero to make a risky business decision that would set off yet more plot complications, but by the time I reach that point I know that this particular man wouldn't be so foolish; so I have to alter the plot, make some other complication occur, or invent jolly good reasons to make him take that risky decision despite himself.

In a romantic suspense book, my hero became so unpleasant that both my heroine and I fell out of love with the beast. I might have toned him down by rewriting some scenes, but that would also have removed a deal of the drama and, besides, the man had reasons for being the way he was — all bitter and twisted because of the past life I'd built up for him. That particular man *would* have behaved in that way and therefore he was wrong for my heroine. Since in real life women do fall for the wrong men at times, I let it happen in my book. Fortunately, a rather nice 'other man' loitered on the sidelines of the plot; he turned out to be a much better prospect — I made sure of that! I built up his part in the earlier chapters, so that when the time came he could step in and provide the happy ending which all such books demand. Since the mystery element of the plot concerned the smuggling of fake works of art, the romantic hiccup also suggested the title: *Counterfeit Love*.

One of the joys of writing, for me, is finding out what's going to happen next. It may sound absurd, but I never know *exactly* how each scene will work out. One character may say something offensive, to which another flares up, and suddenly there's a full-scale row going, which I hadn't planned at all.

Or, conversely, two characters come up with the beginnings
of a private joke which will recur between them through the
book.

In *The Clouded Land*, Kate, just arrived from Germany,
asks what are the 'land ironclads' her uncle has just mentioned
and he says: *'Haven't you read any of Wells's books?'* The plot
thread here involves the early stages of military tanks, so this
conversation is RELEVANT, but as I wrote the scene it
occurred to me that Kate might not have heard of H. G. Wells.
She has, however, met the family lawyer, whose name, I realized, also happened to be Wells; so her logical response was:

> *'Books?' I was confused. 'I didn't know he was a writer.'*
>
> *'Of course he is! Surely, even in Germany, you—'*
>
> *'I thought he was a lawyer.'*
>
> *Uncle Frank peered at me as if I had turned blue, then a sudden
> blast of laughter exploded from him. 'Not Oliver Wells, dunderhead!
> Herbert G. Wells. The Time Machine, The Argonauts of the Air, The
> Land Ironclads . . . No?'*
>
> *'I've never heard of him.'*

From then on, she and her uncle have a running joke over
the name Wells, which points up their warm relationship and,
I like to think, lends a lightness here and there to the bleakness
of the World War One background.

Such unplanned moments mean that your players are becoming real. Just be careful not to let them take complete control
and end up in Wigan when you wanted them in Jamaica.

Of course, *you* may be able to write a complete synopsis
and stick to it with no trouble. If so, do so. My best way is
my best way – *your* best way you must discover for yourself.

Novelist John Braine said that all fiction contains a 'moment
of disbelief', a point when the author is forced to compromise

plausibility in order to bring the plot to a satisfactory conclusion. The trick lies in the way you handle that moment, whether you have the skill to cover the cracks so that they're barely visible, or leave them so wide that even the least critical of readers can detect them. Thank goodness most readers want only to be entertained – they don't sit down to criticize a book, they want to enjoy it. But we, as writers, owe it to ourselves to look more closely at the work of others, in order to train ourselves to avoid some of the pitfalls. Have you ever watched a film, enjoyed it, but later thought, 'Hang on a minute! How come...? What happened to...? They never explained...' If you have, then you've spotted the kind of cracks I'm talking about. Maybe they don't matter, so long as the story, while in progress, keeps you absorbed and willingly *suspending* your disbelief. But if you do note faults, and can also say, 'The author could have made it more believable if she'd done so-and-so, cut this, changed that, added something else...' Ah, *now* you're becoming a constructive critic.

The circular route

As mentioned for articles, above, a method of blending your work into a satisfying whole is to connect the end to the beginning in some way. This works with both fiction and non-fiction. As a simple example, a journalist reviewing the papers on TV began by saying, 'Isn't politics wonderful?' and went on to recount some bizarre political stories from the morning's news, ending with, 'As I said – isn't politics wonderful?' The trick is not new; but it's effective.

A short story begins: *Look ... I don't know why you keep coming to me. It had nothing to do with me. I warned him. I did warn him, time and time again. But you know what kids are like these days. Never listen.* Titled 'Joe's Story', this develops into a modern parable on the life of Jesus, told by his hapless parent to an anonymous journalist. It ends *I'll say it one last time – it had nothing to do with me. He wasn't my son, but I did my best for him and if I'd had my way he'd have been a decent, respectable, useful member of society. But he never would listen to me. I did warn him. Time and time again I warned him. I kept telling him he'd never change the world.* Which rounds it off nicely by bringing it right back to its beginning, almost in the same words, and adding that ironic final punch.

In a novel, the same device worked by having the main character return, in Chapter One, to the scene of earlier traumas with unfinished business to settle. Chapter Two went back in time to the beginning of the story, whose telling took up the rest of the book, leaving a final chapter which saw the woman complete her quest, thus circling back to the beginning.

You can probably think up a dozen variations to this device, which can be used in almost any piece of writing. It lends a pleasing roundness to your work.

Chapter endings and length

Should chapters end at cliff-hanging points of page-turnability? Two schools of thought vie for honours here:

a) make the break in the middle of a scene, at a point of nail-biting tension which has your reader so involved she simply has to turn the page to read on; or

b) stop at a pleasant breathing space, the end of a scene, the end of a day, so that the reader can safely set the book aside until another time.

Which is right? Yet again, there is no absolute 'right' way. It depends on type of book, type of scene, type of effect you're after . . . *You* decide.

How long should your chapters be? Well, how long is a 'short while', or even a 'long while'? Make your chapters as long as is suitable for what you're writing.

If there *is* an average, it's probably around six thousand words. An average book of 75,000 words probably divides into ten or twelve chapters; 200,000 words could be thirty chapters – though it might equally well be forty, or eighteen.

Because of the need to have peaks and troughs in the flow of a novel, you may find your story falls naturally into sections, roughly equal. My advice is, don't worry too much about it. Don't try to get them all exactly the same length. Several pages longer or shorter than the mean, even the odd chapter comprising only a page or two . . . If your story warrants it, do it.

RECAP

- Don't skimp on research. If in doubt about a fact, check it.
- Bear in mind the underlying framework of your prose.
- Main plot types: dispute, choice or realization.
- Work to a tight synopsis or use the loose organic method – your choice.
- To round off a pleasing 'shape', can you link the end to the beginning?

Exercise: Write. Write. Write.

10 · Tying Up the Ends

And so, as the sun sinks slowly in the west . . .

A good ending is almost as important as a good beginning. Almost, because if you've drawn your reader with you this far then you've done your job, but you might as well leave him sighing with pleasure, or perhaps regretting that it's all finished. What you hope NOT to do is make him say, 'What a let-down!' or 'What a cheat!'

This section will be brief. So should your ending be. The shorter the piece, the more succinct the finale. Just as aspiring writers tend to **start too soon** in their story, so they often **end too late**, running on after everything relevant has been said. Relevant – that word again. It seems to have become the motif of this book.

However, although you should end as neatly as possible, tying up all ends, avoid rushing it. Your reader wants everything to be explained, fully and satisfactorily. If you can, save some final surprise until the end – which means the very last line, especially in a short piece.

How did our friend Cassandrina Dustworthy do it?

When Jim came round after several awful days when his poor mother had been driven nearly frantic with worry, he was in bed with a nurse beside him, who told him sadly with tears in her eyes that poor Fiona was tragically dead.

"That's tragic", thought Jim sadly to himself. It will teach me to mend my ways. And it did.

It was the best Christmas present Emily Cartwright ever had.

The last sentence does neatly sum up the whole; so, as finales go, it could be worse. If only a better story had preceded it!

By now, I hope, you can see the faults of repetition and tautology in this extract. (If you can't, go back to Chapter One and start again, you haven't been listening!) The phrase *in bed with a nurse* . . . will make some readers snigger; VP jumps about all over the place; and exactly what was the best Christmas present Emily ever had? *It* is too unspecific.

And how I wish Mrs D. would get her punctuation right! Sorry to bang on about it, but a generous seasoning of mistakes like this is infuriating for an editor. It's simplest not to put any quote marks round thoughts: use quotes only for spoken words. If you *are* going to use them, you have the problem of differentiating thought from words said aloud, and most publishing houses prefer to use only one style of quote marks – single or double. Why give yourself that headache? But, whatever you do, you must be consistent: *"It will teach me to mend my ways."* That's part of his thought, too, so if the first bit has quotes this needs them. And that first comma should be *inside* the quotes, not after them. And *And it did* ought to be on a new line, except that it's another authorial comment. And . . . Oh, I give up! We know what the author is trying to say, but she doesn't say it very well, does she? On the other hand, it is brief and to the point, as all endings should be.

Examples

Do you recall the story about Eric the war-time choirboy who couldn't join his friend David in the duet on Christmas day?

Here's how the rough draft ends, after Mother tells David that Eric has been killed by the doodlebug:

'I, I . . .' Words wouldn't come. I picked up the box and ran upstairs to my bedroom and slammed the door.

Eric couldn't have been killed – I had seen him, after the bomb dropped.

I slowly undid the box. If it hadn't been Eric, who else could it have been?

As I took the lid off the box I instantly knew it had been Eric. It was his train set, which had been his favourite toy. He'd known I'd always wanted one.

And that's the end.

Here again, we know what the author is trying to say, but it could have been expressed in a better way. He's still cutting too many corners, don't you agree? How would *you* have done it?

This is how it eventually finished, after rewrites:

I rushed to my room and slammed the door behind me as I fought to hold back tears. Then I looked down at the package Eric had thrust at me before he left so suddenly, something wrapped in an often-used and precious paper bag. I still didn't believe it. He couldn't have been killed. I spoke to him after the bomb dropped. Unless . . .

The bag contained a battered shoebox. Inside it was Eric's railway engine, which he had sworn never to part with, 'until,' as he had always said, 'until the day I die.'

On Christmas Day the choir and congregation sang carols to celebrate the birth of our Lord, and to wish 'a speedy end to the conflict'.

I sang, 'In the Bleak Midwinter', only for Eric.

The first ending was *too* brief. The second version is, I feel, far more involving and moving. The addition of the last couple of sentences rounds it nicely back to the beginning. Yes?

——————— o ———————

Ending a travel article extolling the delights of Italy's Riviera of Flowers, the author writes:

... This place will make you feel a million dollars.

I could continue to extol the joys of the Italian Riviera, but I hope I have whetted your appetite to travel to this enchanting area of Italy yourself. I know you will not be disappointed. I have travelled there many times and I always find something new to see and come home feeling rejuvenated, vowing to return as soon as possible.

We could cut that last paragraph with no loss, I think; it adds nothing new. Would you advise also finding a way to avoid the rather trite *feel a million dollars*? Can *you* think of a better phrase?

——————— o ———————

After a quarrel, a man returns home late, and drunk, to find his wife weeping. She's been worried sick about him, she says. He's slightly mollified by this, but as they talk she blurts out that she's been having an affair; her lover has just phoned to say he's staying with his wife. So ... *Brian looked into her eyes and bitterly realized her tears had not been for him.* Brief story, brief ending. Nice one.

——————— o ———————

Under 'author's tone of voice' we glanced at a tale told by a woman to her best friend, Sylvia, over several Christmas gins.

She recounts a colourful and humorous story about her enforced stay in an isolated monastery high in the Andes, where the thirty-one resident monks are under a vow of silence. The woman is obliged to remain in her room during the time she's there — her husband has been injured in a fall and they're waiting to be rescued. The only person she sees is one young novice, Fernando, who can't speak to her and who hardly dares look at her. However, every night of the thirty nights she's there, he comes to her room, in pitch darkness, and, much to her relish, makes passionate love to her. After a month, a llama-cart arrives to transport the wounded man back down the mountain. Says the *raconteuse* . . .

I was all choked up. Marv was cussing at the Indians while they loaded him on the cart and I was ashamed of his language. I couldn't bear to look at Fernando, so I watched the monks file slowly away, thirty of them.

I guess Fernando just couldn't help himself. He whispered, 'I'm sorry you have to go today. It would have been my turn tonight.'

You gotta smile. Thirty-one of them altogether and I had to leave before the thirty-first night. There they were, heads down, like as peas in a pod and . . . Sylvia? Where you going? Sylvia? . . .

Oh, my, she's gone. I knew she didn't have no sense of humour. Some people will believe anything.

This rough version tends to belabour the joke. After some thought and discussion, the author edited it thus:

. . . so I watched the monks file slowly away, heads down, like as peas in a pod.

I guess Fernando just couldn't help himself. He whispered, 'I'm sorry you have to go today. It would have been my turn tonight.'

Sylvia? Where you going? Sylvia? . . .

Oh, my, she's gone. I knew she didn't have no sense of humour. Some people will believe anything.

I'm still unsure whether those last two lines are necessary. What do *you* think?

————— o —————

The story told by the puppy (see Chapter Four) begins:

It's the old lady again, standing at our shop window. I first noticed her the other week, looking at me and the others scampering about our play pen. Every day since then she's stopped to watch our antics. Today I think I'll give her my full repertoire of party tricks. Rolling over, chasing my own tail, nipping my sisters' ears, and the finale of the plaintive adoring expression . . . Oh, she's gone.

It stays amusingly inside the puppy's VP as customers come and go. It's Christmas Eve and one by one other pets are sold, including the pup's two sisters, leaving him alone. He's not sorry for himself, but he gets a little wistful when the shop owner starts to close up early – he's heard her say she's going to a party. Then, at the last minute, the old lady appears again. She tells the shop owner that she's recently lost her own dog and would love to have the puppy to replace him, but, oh dear, she can't afford the price.

'Squawk, squawk.'
Percy, put a sock in it, my future is about to be decided. Oh no, Grandma's shaking her head. Give her a discount! Too late, she's at the door. There goes my last chance.
Arrgggh, I hate being picked up by the scruff of the neck. Why am I being held out to her?
'I can't take your money. You have him as my Christmas present. Just make sure you buy his dog food here.'
I don't understand humans. When I show my teeth it's because I'm angry, when they do it, it's because they're happy. I haven't

seen this bit before, though: her eyes are leaking. Hmmm, her arms are warm and cuddly.

A pleasantly sentimental ending for a Christmas story with a difference. Notice how, by starting with the old lady peering in the window the author was able to round it off nicely with puppy and old lady united. I liked the way the little dog described her tears, too. Did you? Or was it *too* sloppy for your taste?

However long the story, you should keep the ending concise. Once the main narrative thread is cut, your reader doesn't want to plough on through a morass of explanations of how the characters went on and did this, that or the other. If your story requires considerable space to tie up ends, be sure to keep some narrative hooks in place, some extra tension, a last-minute hiccup: save some last surprise until the end.

In this extract, from a long novel telling the story of Boudicca (*The People of the Horse*, W. H. Allen, 1987), the ending had to accord with history, which recounts that the great warrior queen died; what became of her two daughters is not recorded. In this version, after their final disastrous battle, a few of Boudicca's people return to their old home. Among them is the queen's older daughter, Rhiannon.

Boudicca's death is probably the real climax but, because we've been watching events through Rhiannon's eyes for some while, her story too has to reach a conclusion. Some surprises remain: in the last few pages, Rhiannon comes near to losing her baby son under the knife of a fanatical priestess (the cult of the Earth/Moon Goddess is a strong motif woven through the book); then the arrival of some Roman soldiers threatens the safety of both herself and her baby. That danger, too, is averted, thanks to other plot-threads which now reach their own conclusion. On the very last page, the People of the Horse are granted a real sign of hope when a group of hunters returns, bringing home a herd of young horses . . .

. . . Among them, to Rhiannon's delight, was the young stallion Starson, first of the new breed, sire of the future.

In delight, the men rode wildly round and round, driving the horses before them. The beat of hooves sounded good to Rhiannon, the toss of manes made her laugh, and she saw her son's eyes light with pleasure at the sight of the animals. Nion, too, was warrior-bred, she thought as she hugged him for sheer joy.

She felt the Goddess whisper along the wind, no longer cold Caridwen but strong, sure, lusty Epona, the White Mare, Queen of the Winds – She who had guided Rhiannon since childhood. Now She returned in the thud of hooves and the surge of hope, bringing with Her a promise of peace.

Rhiannon thought of all her friends – those who remained and those who had gone before. All of them would hold a place in the history of Boudicca, last warrior queen of Icenia. The bards had gone, who might have sung her story, but though Rhiannon had few poetic skills she promised herself she would compose the song for her children and their children – a song to be sung around the fires in warriors' hall of a winter's night, that all should remember.

> *'Let the song be of Boudicca,*
> *of her life and of her spirit;*
> *which is fled with skeins of wild geese*
> *to the back of the north wind;*
> *though she dwells in the Glass Castle,*
> *beyond the sight of mortals,*
> *she remains in burnished memory,*
> *one with earth and sky and water;*

with the Maid, her older daughter,
one with Thee, threefold Goddess.'

This book was prefaced by a poem; so it ends with one. Boudicca is gone, but among her people her legend will live on.

And it has, hasn't it? Two thousand years on, her name still rings heroic bells in our race memory.

Do you find this method of ending appropriate to the theme?

Counting words

As you were writing, you should have borne in mind the length you were aiming for, to suit your market: 2500 for an average short story; 60,000 to 75,000 for the average book; 120,000 or more for a saga. (NB: These are round figures intended only as a guide – always check the current requirements of your particular market.)

To count words for publication take an average of words-per-line (count the words on ten different lines, add them together, and divide by ten); then count lines per page (each page should have the same number of lines); multiply those together to find how many words per page; then multiply by the number of pages.

With a book-length MS, count every page as full: don't allow for chapter beginnings or endings – the printer wants to know how many complete pages the book is going to take.

For example: with normal type or print, you may have an average of 13 words per line, with 29 lines per page: $13 \times 29 = 377$ words per page; so if you complete 402 pages you can estimate your wordage as $377 \times 402 = 151,554$. Which you could round down to 'approx. 150,000'.

For short stories and articles, gain a more accurate estimate by counting the exact number of lines. On a full page they should be the same as for a book – say 29, as above. If your piece runs to page seven, it will have five full pages of 29 lines, with, probably, fewer lines on page 1 (to allow space for your heading) and on page 7 (where the story ends before the last line). So line count is $5 \times 29 = 145 + 26 + 23 = 194$ lines in the story. Multiply that by your average words per line: $194 \times 13 = 2522$. On your title page, you then put 'About 2500 words'.

By the time you've completed your rough draft, you will have some idea of whether you need to cut some words or to add some. Cutting may be painful, but when well done it's *always* beneficial. Padding is not so easy; by definition, it's adding extraneous material, but if you add words *of sufficient interest* they should enhance the whole. Never, ever, shove in a few paragraphs of waffle just to bulk it out; better leave it a little short than add flab.

RECAP

- Endings should be suitable, satisfying and succinct.
- Your piece should be the right length for its market.

Exercise: If you haven't already finished a piece of writing, do so now. See how good *you* are at tying up ends.

Study endings: read good books and see the way other authors have done it. And look again at your own work, if you have some samples finished. Were the endings tight and satisfying? Could they have been improved? Made more concise?

Think about words. Eat, sleep, talk and breathe writing.

11 · Reviewing and Self-editing

Be your own prose doctor

'Another chapter? But we've just done endings. What else is there?'

Thought your job was finished? Sorry. As the song says, we've only just begun. You've done the hardest work, created that raw material, mined that diamond; now you come to the final stages, where you cut, hone and polish your gem, ready for the world to see. Some people find this a chore: to me, it's the most enjoyable part of the job.

Before you begin reviewing, though, take a break. You've earned it. Walk down a leafy lane, cycle the moors, weed your garden, or go off and cruise the Pacific, whatever your lifestyle allows. Let the manuscript rest, too. Distance yourself from it, forget it if you can; you'll see it more objectively when you come back to it. You'll find you can never view it with a completely fresh eye, except perhaps after years have gone by and you've totally forgotten it, but who wants to wait that long? So, do the best you can to put it out of your mind, at least for a while. Perhaps, remembering the advice to write something every day, you could start planning your next piece.

When you feel ready, get the work out and read it through again. Critically. Resist the temptation to wallow in self-congratulation, seeing only your baby's charm and cuteness.

It will have warts, and freckles, probably terminal acne. It may even have two heads, or only one leg. Notice the faults. Cure them if you can. How? Well, let's find out . . .

Final arbiter – you, the author

Before we launch into this final furlong, I must emphasize that there is no 'right way' of doing these things. We're not talking mathematics, where a sum is either right or wrong: writing is a matter of judgement. What suits you, what suits your style, what suits the kind of piece you're hoping to produce: all those things will influence your final choice. Where I suggest editorial changes, I show one possible way of tackling the problem. There may well be several other ways, each equally effective. Look for them. Think how *you* would do it. How you edit your own work is, in the end, entirely **your decision**.

A cutting tool is your best friend now. Eliminate all excess verbiage – which means everything that isn't doing a job of some kind. Make sure every word has **relevance**. Remember, the shorter the piece, the more spare and well-pruned your prose must be. But even in the longest saga every word must have a function, adding to the reader's knowledge, carrying the story forward, colouring the picture, filling the senses, enlarging on character, heightening tension, providing information, sending telegraphs, intriguing, interesting or mystifying the reader.

Don't be tempted to pad with verbosity, don't write for effect or leave in irrelevancies because you like the way you've written them. On the other hand, don't pare so much that you chop away *necessary* words, as the authors of some of our examples have done. You're writing full, rich English prose, not notes, scraps and fragments.

Trust your instinct.

Four readers

To focus your critical faculties, bear in mind four possible readers:

1. **The Colonel**. He's a pedant, thinks English should be written as it was when he went to school. For him, have grammar, punctuation, vocabulary and syntax as accurate as you can. If you deviate from current norms, be ready to argue your case when challenged.

2. **Aunt Freda**. Being an interested, lively, inquisitive type, Freda is happy to read your work and hopes to enjoy it. But she'll notice anything that strikes her as illogical, or improbable, and will tell you about it – hoping to help, of course. Write about picking runner beans in June and she will point out that runner beans don't crop until late July. For her sake, pay attention to plausibility.

3. **Cousin Simon** is lazy. He likes a good read, but he doesn't want to work too hard at it and he can be a little slow on the uptake. If you've left too many holes for him to fill in, or jumped about from place to place without good transitions, he'll be confused and give up. He calls for clarity.

4. Finally, there's **Silly Gilly** from next door. Gilly has an eye for the comical, the incongruous, the absurd. If you've written, *She sat with her head in her hands and her eyes on the floor*, Gilly will fall off her chair laughing. So watch out for unintentional howlers.

Imagine these readers standing behind you, looking over your shoulder, every time you read through your work. **The editor on whose desk your story is about to land might be one of them!**

Creating effects – the rhythm method

Notice the rhythm of your prose, the pattern you've created. Is it varied enough, or does it drone on, paragraph after paragraph with sentences all composed alike? Have you used your skill to tighten or lessen tension as appropriate? Consider this:

The sunlight glistened on the window pane. Katy watched it. It seemed to dance and sparkle on the cobwebs. Katy had seen that sparkle before, in her mother's eyes. Her mother had died two months before. The doctor said she felt no pain, but Katy did. Her mother was the only person who seemed to care about her. Her father was in Scotland on business and didn't even come down for the funeral. Katy blamed him for her mother's death.

From a sixteen-year-old this is not bad, showing promise of better things to come. At present the writer uses too many short, choppy sentences, all beginning with the main clause: this creates a staccato effect which is not entirely harmonious with the subject matter. Repetition of *her mother* and the name *Katy* could be avoided, too, don't you think? And possibly we could try altering *Her mother was ... Her father was ...* in consecutive sentences.

Contrast the style of that last piece with this:

They knocked down the house last week and all trace of it is gone now, except perhaps a garden path and some bushes we used to play in – games like Jungles, Cowboys and Indians, Secret Garden and straightforward Hide and Seek. In the name of progress and road widening and development, a home that knew joy and sadness, life and death, hope and despair, but, above all, security and continuity for sixty eventful years, has gone. The changing colours and patterns of the fields have been swallowed in the gradual creeping encroachment of expanding villages and housing estates, which eventually sentenced the house to death.

Can you see how long, leisured sentences actually add to the atmosphere of regret and melancholia? It wouldn't have the same effect if it had been written in short sentences, would it? If I were editing, I might ask for a trim of the second to last line — *gradual, creeping, encroachment* and *expanding* all have much the same meaning. How about *in the creeping encroachment of villages and housing estates, which . . .* I'd keep *creeping encroachment*, because I like the image it raises, and I like the alliteration in the repeated '*cr*' sound. What do you think?

A further contrast:

I lunged for the reins, thinking to halt the pony. Basil fended me off. In desperation I threw myself at him, grasping again for the reins. We struggled fiercely. Close as lovers. Deadly as enemies. I clawed for his face. I remember his breath on my cheek, the feel of his clothing, the odour of his skin.

The rest is only impressions. The bridge racing closer. The river, glinting dark. Bushes tangled thickly along the banks. Out of those bushes, something white, startling in the darkness. Huge wings flapping. A swan! The pony screaming, hooves pawing the air. The trap, slewing round, bucking under me. Tossing me free. The sky revolving around me. The swan flapping away. Thunder cracking. Wood splintering. Basil's cry.

And then nothing.

Nothing.

Here, short choppy sentences — many of them not even proper sentences but fragments (Did you notice? Did it matter?) — combine to give a feeling of the runaway trap, the girl's frantic efforts to save herself. The writer has broken the rules of grammar *knowingly*, to create an effect. Does it work? How was it for you?

Don't be passive — activate!

One of the most frequent flaws among less practised stylists is the over-use of passive language, which, instead of sparkling and scintillating, flattens the prose and wearies the reader with tedium. Passivity comes when you have an object (or person) **having something done to it**; in the more interesting, active style of writing, an object (or person) is **doing something** — taking action, not being acted upon. In its simplest form: *The radio was switched on by the boy* is passive; *The boy switched on the radio* is active.

Passive: *The child was put into the car.* Active: *The man put the child into the car.*

Passive: *His hair was now flecked with grey, but his smile was as disarming as ever.* Active: *Flecks of grey showed in his dark hair, but his smile still disarmed her.*

See if you can spot, and see ways of correcting, the passivity in the following:

1. *Even to one used to the inconveniences of prison, Newgate came as a very nasty shock. It was built around one of the entrance gates to the city of London, the New Gate, which for centuries had served as a hold for criminals, but which in time had grown and spread to include the area called the Old Bailey as well. Entrance was gained to the prison through the gate itself.*

The portcullis was raised, as it probably always was, and Roger's impression as he was escorted in was of dirty faded grandeur, of sculpted stonework embellishing windows and walls and stone figures in niches. The ornamentation was at strong variance to Roger's own expectations of a place which was notorious, the mere mention of which struck terror into the soul of any man.

There was little time to admire the view. Roger was . . .

2. *As the buggy rolled out of town, the morning train drew in. Only three people alighted, and it was perhaps as well that Welden Granger was still peacefully asleep and unable to note their arrival. Olivia was tight-lipped, as she had been throughout the journey. Amelia, who was a bad traveller and had hardly slept since leaving Boston, was pale and hollow-eyed. Marcus was sweating profusely. He was sure that this trip was unwise and had degenerated into a bundle of open nerve ends.*

3. *The submarine was forgotten as all eyes turned forward. A group of dolphins far to our left were diving into the oncoming waves . . .*

4. *The climate in this part of Italy is temperate all the year round as it is sheltered by the Alps and the Appennines. This means that one of the main sources of income for the region is market gardening, one of the main crops being carnations, which are exported all over Europe. Greenhouses are to be seen all along the coast, filled with beautiful specimens of all colours. Olive oil is another important export and the countryside is full of gnarled olive trees which have been producing olives for years.*

5. First sentences from successive sections of a story:

He was brought out of his thoughts by the sudden crying of the baby . . . Henry and Madge were contentedly picking strawberries when . . . The dining room was loud with argument . . . The atmosphere was at once apparent to the perceptive Madge . . . It was half-time in the football match on TV. Henry and his son were indulging in a technical discussion . . . Madge was mildly surprised when her daughter's usual rush for the bus . . .

Comments: In all of these examples, the main problem is over-reliance on the verb 'to be', or parts of it: 'is', 'are', 'was', 'were', 'be', 'being', and so on. Count how many times these words are used. Do you see how it distances us from the action, makes it less immediate? This is passive writing. If you find it in your own work, try to liven it up.

Specific points:

Extract 1. The first paragraph, while giving information, doesn't paint much of a picture. The author has done her research, but hasn't translated it into good fiction. That *very nasty shock* is a touch Blytonesque. But the whole thing needs recasting, putting soundly inside the viewpoint of the hapless Roger.

Entrance was gained . . .is such an uninteresting way of saying it: entrance was gained by whom? This is a story, so we want to know how these surroundings affect our hero. Why not something like, *The guards dragged him through the gate, under the raised portcullis* . . . Action, you see – somebody **doing** something.

In the second paragraph, was, was, was, was . . . It must be changed. We do have a little more detail here, but it gets a bit convoluted: *The ornamentation was at strong variance to Roger's own expectations of a place which was notorious* . . . Again, we're distanced, not seeing through Roger's perceptions but viewing from a detached VP, and the language is awkward. If it means that the prison wasn't as he had imagined it, why doesn't it just say so? And what of *the mere mention of which struck terror into the soul of any man*? Isn't that a cliché – or is it two?

The author doesn't appear to have a grasp of how the place looked and sounded, or what her protagonist must have been feeling as he was dragged to his incarceration. At least, if it's clear in her own mind, she hasn't passed the picture on to us.

Extract 2. Again the over-use of that boring word 'was' (it's a useful little beast, but don't flog it to death). There's an error of syntax in the last sentence, too, since the *trip* had not degenerated into *a bundle of open nerve ends* (another cliché?). Suggest: *Sure that this trip was unwise, he had degenerated into* . . . which at least gets rid of one of those wretched wases.

Extract 3. Distance and inertia again. Suggest: *We forgot the submarine as a group of dolphins to our left dived into the oncoming waves* . . .

Extract 4. Again, too heavy reliance on the verb 'to be' and its various participles – *is, are, being, have been,* even an actual *to be* – ten occurrences in just seven lines. Instead of making us long to visit the place, this only states guidebook facts in a somewhat stolid manner. *All the year round* is redundant; *one of the main* is repeated in consecutive lines; *beautiful specimens of all colours* is another of those vague adjectival phrases which give no real picture. That sentence could be recast: *All along the coast, sunlight glitters on acres of greenhouses full of flowers, burgeoning in scarlets, pinks and* . . . (whatever colours there may be).

Extract 5. If you catch yourself *frequently* writing sentences like these, try to change at least some of them. They're perfectly acceptable, grammatically, but they don't make lively prose. Use too many of them and your work becomes leaden. Always prefer the active voice, where possible.

Over-ornamentation

Look again for excessive adjectives and adverbs; cut words and phrases that reiterate a thought unnecessarily; and weed out clichés.

Below, I offer a few examples with the ornamental, redundant or clichéd words highlighted. See how the essential meaning of the sentences remains unchanged if you take out the descriptive flourishes. Then decide for yourself which of the marked words are vital, which could be cut out entirely, and which might be expressed more vividly.

1. *The _full_ moon was playing hide and seek with the stars, _behind the few rapidly moving clouds_, bathing the _whole_ farmyard in a _silvery_ glow as George took his _last_ look around before bedtime. As he _peacefully_ smoked his pipe _on this beautiful Sunday evening_, _quietly planning the week ahead_, his _slightly impaired_ hearing picked up the _unmistakable_ drone of a _dreaded_ Heinkel. _Looking skyward_, trying to catch a glimpse of the _enemy_ bomber, a sight met his eyes which struck chill through his very soul.* (Is this last phrase too much of a cliché? Would you alter it, too? To what?)

2. *Whatever mysteries barred my thoughts _like a protecting veil_, I knew I had never before been on this road. As I walked in the _September_ air, the _climbing_ sun dispersed the _last of the early morning_ mist and, _as if for my eyes alone_, the countryside paraded its _golden mellowed_ cloak of autumn. The _lush_ grass that verged _both sides_ of the road _was heavy with dew_ and bearded the _irregular_ hedgerows of _broad and narrow leaf_ greenery which gave way in places to the _thorny_ bearers of _ripening_ blackberries.*

3. *His mother, Violet, a _waspy bay Shire_ mare _with four white feet and a white blaze upon her forehead_, was already up on her feet, _excitedly_ licking her _new-born_ foal, while _softly_ whinnying, _deep_ in her _cavernous_ throat, as she _carefully_ cleaned his _pulsating_ nostrils, his mouth, eyes and ears before turning her attention to his _steaming_ underbelly . . .*

No, there's no answer at the back of the book — there's no 'right' way of doing it. It's **author's choice**, a matter of taste and style, but if these were my pieces I would cut some of the marked words. Which ones? Well, which do you think we could do without?

On some occasions, ornamentation works to **enhance** a piece. Think of Kipling's *great, grey-green, greasy Limpopo River* ... His 'Just-So' Stories were for children, intentionally humorous, but if you speak that line aloud you can almost *feel* the river sliding slimily through the jungle, helped by all those lovely alliterative adjectives. You may be writing a story that warrants the same kind of verbal artifice. You alone can tell. So long as you *know* you're doing it, and so long as you know *why* . . .

As always, the last test is **relevance**.

Viewpoint

Keep a sharp eye out for shifts of viewpoint, such as in this passage:

> *He used always to enjoy the walk home from the station on Friday evenings, but recently it hadn't been the same. His pride and pleasure in his immaculate, if somewhat unimaginative, garden remained the same as ever. His deep, almost maudlin tenderness for little Rosie could never change. But lately, when he thought of Kathy, whom he still loved, the faint vertical lines between his eyebrows deepened perceptibly, and he experienced a feeling of something very like foreboding.*

Did you spot it? *the faint vertical lines ... deepened perceptibly*? To whose perceptions? Can't be the VP character's, unless he's constantly staring into a mirror.

Or this:

> *More expense! the rector thought, trying hard not to let exasperation show on his amiable face. His thoughts were centred on the*

*enormous problem of where to find the funding required for the
extensive repairs to his church. He seemed unaware that it was
still raining as he walked across the green.*

He might try not to let his exasperation show, but he
wouldn't think of his own face as being amiable, nor would
he think he 'seemed' to be aware – he's either aware or he's
not. The middle sentence is verbose and could be sharpened:
*His thoughts centred on the problem of finding funds for extensive
repairs to his church.*

Small tip: Try cutting out the word 'the' whenever you can,
as in the example above – *the funding, the repairs* . . .

Syntax

Precision with words is essential if you want to convey your
meaning with true clarity.

A news bulletin reported: *Jimmy Carter's highly publicized
meetings with Kim Il-Sung gave him a higher profile than ever before.*
By 'him', it meant the North Korean leader, as became evident
later in the piece. But it *seems* to mean Jimmy Carter, because
he's named first. Swap the names and the meaning is clearer.

Another newscaster announced: *He snatched his daughter
from her grandparents' home, where she had been staying on New
Year's Eve.* Journalists learn to put the main punch first, in this
case 'He snatched her . . .' But the child hadn't been staying
with her grandparents *only* on New Year's Eve, so the next
bulletin rephrased it: *On New Year's Eve, he snatched his daughter from her grandparents' home, where she had been staying.*
(Note where the apostrophes go.)

The news is a rich source of solecisms like this, I guess
because it's written in a hurry. Often, by the time the item's
repeated, it has been corrected.

Take: *A young friend of mines father, was a policeman*. In this the words are all back to front and the punctuation haywire: the comma after *father* shouldn't be there, and *friend of mine's* would need this apostrophe, if it were proper English. Surely the sentence should read, *The father of a young friend of mine was a policeman*?

When using **pronouns** such as 'he', 'she', and 'it', be careful of their placement. Mrs Dustworthy gave us a few instances of 'how not to' in her story. We had: *She had hated them ever since her brother was so tragically killed during the blackout when he had been a messenger on the staff of the famous Monty. Now, he had been a fine young man, one of the best ...* Who had been a fine young man? Monty? Later she writes: *Then suddenly a dog ran out. Jim slammed on his brakes but sadly hit him and he was dead before he hit the ground*. Who was dead: Jim, or the dog? Minor points, but Aunt Freda will spot them, Cousin Simon will be confused and Silly Gilly will howl with laughter.

Be alert for **muddled thinking**, as in: *So sharp were the arguments* [about washing up] *that it was ordained that we were to do all of it, each by herself, washing, drying and putting away*. Come again? The first half of this sentence is passive, the rest is clumsy and gives itself the added problem of getting the plural *we* tangled with the singular *each ... herself*. How about: *We argued so much that mother decreed we should take it in turns to do it all – washing, drying and putting away*.

Or take this:

One of those who had lately become a regular was Jan Abbott and, despite myself, I find my mind and thoughts revolving around her image. She is tall and dark, quiet, but with an enquiring mind, and I had helped her choose books to read from the new stock on the shelves. In fact I have one she had asked me to obtain, and I know she was interested in, what better to improve acquaintance and deliver it in person, on this dreary end to a routine day. I decided to drop it off on my way home, having established she was divorced and probably very lonely by the amount of reading she consumed. I'm forty-five, and our marriage a good one, if some-what routine. Monday night squash, Tuesday gym class, Wednes-day friends round, etc. etc., all good and livable, but what? Yes! dull, and tonight I feel in need of a lift and a mild adventure, if it proved into the unknown then I'll back out quickly, but here goes, this is the street, and here is the house.

We can't tell where we're supposed to be, or when; the tenses are all adrift and the information is stuck in anyhow, words thrown down without shape or form. If you can't see the flaws without my explaining them, perhaps you should choose another pastime. How would *you* rewrite it to make it more coherent?

The right word in the right place

Have you chosen the **correct word** to express the thought, even to your reader Aunt Freda? If you write *The dog literally flew out of the door* Freda will want to know why you didn't mention before that this dog had wings. 'Yes, dear, I know what you *meant*, but that isn't what you *wrote*.' Be careful with this word 'literally': it means that something actually did happen exactly as you've expressed it. *The lightning literally split the tree down the middle* – the tree really was split in two. But don't say *I was literally gutted when he told me he'd found someone else* – not unless your entrails are hanging out.

Can you cut any wishy-washy, **redundant words** that have crept in without your noticing them, words such as *really, hardly, very, actually, in fact/the fact that . . .* ? Billy Bunter might say '*The weather was really, jolly, awfully, bally cold, actually,*' but unless you're speaking through a character who talks this way, be plain: say *The weather was cold.* Better still, write: *Breath clouded on the air* or similar, using active, lively words that show rather than tell. Don't pussyfoot about with constant prevarications: *almost, nearly, somewhat . . .* Be specific and positive as often as you can. Your work will be better for it.

Certain words tend to be so over-used that they become clichés in themselves. Watch for constant repetitions of tired old verbs: *grinned, chuckled, stared, looked, gazed, frowned, smiled, laughed, realized* and the like, including pet words of your own that may creep in without your noticing. I often find I've acquired a fresh bad verbal habit for every new book! Try to find unusual ways of saying the same old thing. Use your thesaurus (but use it judiciously, and if in doubt check the meaning of the synonym with your dictionary: finding both *incontinent* and *luxurious* under the heading *intemperate* does not mean they're interchangeable!).

Writers of letters to newspapers have a habit of beginning their letters with **dangling participles:** *Being a disabled pensioner . . .* or *Being a dog-owner . . .* or *As a teenager . . .* This is fine, so long as they continue with *I . . .* because such phrases always refer to the noun that immediately follows. Instead, you'll see things like, *Being a disabled pensioner, my garden is full of weeds.* His garden is a disabled pensioner? Or *Being a dog owner, these people who protest about animal mess . . .* (These people are a dog owner?) Or, *As a teenager, the highlight of the school year . . .* (The highlight of the school year was a teenager?) All of these are incorrect.

They might have said, *Because I am a disabled pensioner, my garden . . .* ; *Being a dog owner, I resent the people who protest . . .* ; *When I was a teenager, the highlight . . .*

Likewise:

While harvesting lavender, a bee stung him. (Better: *While he was harvesting . . .* Or, *As he harvested . . .*)

On opening the window, rain poured in. (*When I opened the window . . .*)

Not being train enthusiasts, there was little in the Railway Museum to interest us. (*As we were not train enthusiasts, little . . . interested us.*)

Having heard my story, it was decided to drop charges. (*. . . the police decided to drop charges.*)

Although I've added, in brackets, one method of correcting these, they could be phrased in other, equally grammatical, ways. Depends on context, emphasis and style – you choose.

Writers of blurbs for TV programmes and films commit similar syntactical sins: *Apparently a suicide, Inspector McNulty suspects . . .* (Better: Inspector McNulty suspects that what appeared to be a suicide . . .); *Leo tries to foil the robber who is after his father's car hoping to win approval.* (Hoping to win approval, Leo foils the robber who . . .) Watch out for them. Start your own collection of bloopers.

Another source of problems is the **misplaced modifier,** as in the following sentences:

1. *Candied lavender flowers were, supposedly, a sweet-meat which worked like a charm to provoke love.* The word *supposedly* is the modifier here. In this sentence, it casts doubt on *sweet-meat* when it should logically query *worked like a charm.* Correction: *Candied lavender flowers were a sweet-meat which, supposedly, worked like a charm to provoke love.*

2. *She only said yesterday that she was coming.* This literally means that the only words this person spoke yesterday were that she was coming. What it *intends* to mean is: *She said only yesterday that she was coming.*

Similar snags occur with words like *both*, *either*, *neither*, *not only* . . . Be aware that these hazards lurk, watch out for them and, if in doubt, check with your book of English grammar. The basic rule is that modifiers should be as close as possible to the words they're trying to modify. If they do creep in, your sharp-eyed editor may notice them for you. If not, maybe your reader won't notice, either – except if he's that pedant, the Colonel.

Logic

Not only words, but all your material needs to be presented in logical order. If you're trying to put over a complicated idea, begin with the simplest elements and work up to the most complex. For instance, if your child were to ask where babies come from, would you immediately launch into a lecture on safe sex? Or would you answer simply, 'They grow inside their mummy,' and let him digest that and work out what the next question ought to be, probably months later.

Imagine *yourself* as the questioner and follow the logical sequence of your argument, one fact leading to the next.

In fiction, be sure your scenes themselves are in best order. Sometimes you can create better plots, better dramatic tension, better narrative hooks, by changing the timing of events. Make them happen at the right moment for optimum impact: if the child sees the elf-king *after* she's had a quarrel with her mother, the adults will be more likely to think she's lying in order to get attention, thus creating more conflict.

Also, be consistent: always follow the ground rules you've set up for yourself. If you've created a moonless night, your character won't easily see someone hiding in the wood – unless you add a light of some kind; you can't just forget about the dark because it suits you, you have to think of ways round the problem you've created. Even a way-out fantasy has its own built-in logic: a world where magic occurs must follow its own rules e.g. the good lion Aslan has to die to fulfil the laws of Narnia. Forget this rule and Aunt Freda will be after you.

Avoid being tricksy and deliberately misleading (writing a story about a love affair in which the lovers turn out to be cats, for instance). It never works for long, and looks amateurish. And don't show off your erudition for the sake of it; that, too, becomes obvious to readers and serves only to irritate them.

Whoops!

The Bishop preached a short sermon, much to the delight of the congregation.

The blast was said to have been caused by a build-up of gas by a spokesman.

She died in the house where she was born at the age of 89.

On Easter Sunday, the children laid eggs on the altar.

LAMB BORN TO FARMER WITH FIVE LEGS

This kind of thing will have Silly Gilly rolling on the floor.

Final checks

You've reached the penultimate draft, when all the major editing has been done. Now it's nit-picking time. Have you checked your spelling? Is your punctuation correct? In parentheses (commas, dashes, or brackets which frame parts of sentences) make sure both ends of the frame are in place, and in the *right* place.

Have you checked for tautology, things said twice, facts stated more than once, meaning repeated over again or several ways of saying the same thing all put together at once? Do you need all those adjectives and/or adverbs? Can you strike through any redundant uses of 'the'? What about other small, useless words? What about extraneous sentences? Prune everything that doesn't have a role to play.

Seeing all the tiny flaws at this late stage can be difficult: you need to concentrate; you find yourself seeing what you know *ought* to be there rather than what's actually written. Expect to miss a few mistakes, which, hopefully, your copy-editor will pick up.

The copy-editor, however, is not there to act as co-author. Her main job is to prepare your manuscript for the typesetter, to comply with house style (a publisher's preferred way of producing finished work) and to ensure that translation from type to print runs smoothly. Even so, the copy-editor is a professional; she won't leave in small mistakes she may spot and she will query anything that seems inconsistent. A good copy-editor is the author's invaluable friend − a fresh eye can be useful and none of us is infallible. But do be professional, produce your piece to the best of your ability *before* it reaches the editor. Later emendations should be purely cosmetic. Once in printed proof form, corrections should be kept to a minimum; if you want to rewrite then, you may be sent a bill for the costs incurred.

Anyway, if you leave your MS full of bloopers it won't get as far as the copy-editor's desk. It has a long way to go before it reaches those dizzy heights (see Chapter Twelve).

——————— o ———————

RECAP

- Prefer plain English.
- Bear in mind four readers: the pompous pedant, the earnest enquirer, the lazy lump, and the one with an eye for absurdity.
- Vary the length of sentences. Short and sharp adds tension. Long, languid sentences slow down the pace.
- Avoid starting every sentence with the main clause.
- Prefer the active verb to the passive, the strong to the weak.
- Use adjectives, adverbs and other ornamentation with discretion.
- Check that viewpoint is consistent.
- Study syntax.
- Express thoughts clearly, avoid muddle.
- Are you sure you've used the right word, in the right place, to say exactly what you intended?
- Present your material in logical sequence.
- Make a final painstaking check for small errors and repetitions.

Exercise: Since so many writers weaken their prose by constant application of the verb 'to be', try rewriting the following passage with all parts of that verb replaced by stronger, meatier words and phrases. Turn the sentences around, mix and match them as you please, just leave in the basic facts and as much colour as you feel it needs. To help you, we've marked the words in question. Have fun.

It was a misty, golden September morning. The trees were still green, though some of them were starting to turn brown, and the hedgerows were thick with blackberries which were growing in heavy clumps. As Mike was cycling down into the valley, he heard some women laughing. They were busy in a field, gleaning the corn, while on the opposite side of the road some men were harvesting the runner beans which were growing there.

There were two heavy horses pulling a heavy threshing machine along the lane, and by a cottage gate a woman was pouring milk from her cycle-cart, by means of a ladle, into a great blue jug which was being held by an urchin who was wearing an oversized cap and baggy shorts. There was a woman, presumably she was his mother, who was shouting instructions to him from the end of the path, where she was standing with a baby on her hip.

You'll find one way of editing this demonstrated on page 208.

12 · Off to the Post Office . . .

Don't send broad beans to Billingsgate

By this time you will (won't you?) have studied your market as mentioned in Chapter One. Please do your research in this area thoroughly; however good your MS may be, if you send it to the wrong place it will come back, probably with a polite but uninformative compliment slip. Few publishers have time to write explanatory letters to every hopeful beginner who elects to honour them with his or her work. Indeed, some publishers will not even look at unsolicited submissions: so ensure that your chosen recipient is not one who reads only those pieces he has asked to see.

With non-fiction, both articles and books, you'll be wise to make sure, well in advance, that your subject is of interest to the publisher: send a query letter or a book proposal. Be assured, publishers do not steal ideas. Honestly, they don't. Ten to one your brainchild is not all that original, anyway. And, even if it does promise to break new ground, other writers are too busy with their own ideas to need yours. Besides which, no two people handle ideas in the same way. One of the delights of a creative writing class is that I can give fifteen people the same basic story idea and the result is fifteen totally different stories. So don't be afraid to send queries, to check that the market is ready for your planned piece before you write it. Think of the work you'll save.

When studying your field by looking at books already published, be sure to look at *recent* publications. Just because you have a shelf full of sun-faded books from Hamish Hamilton, don't assume that Hamish Hamilton still wants more of the same. The world of publishing is in constant flux, with takeovers and mergers happening frequently; large conglomerates often have different goals from those their individual component companies had a few years ago. So, rather than looking in libraries, do your market research in book shops – ones which sell *new* books.

If you find that you enjoy the latest books from a particular company, then chances are your taste coincides with that of the current commissioning editor; he (or she) is the person you want to reach since he's the one who will make an offer for your book – you hope. Find out what his name is. How? Ring the publisher's receptionist and ask! Addressing your work to him personally won't guarantee an acceptance, but he may be impressed to see you've taken some trouble and done a bit of sleuthing. That said, bear in mind that editors come and go, sometimes at an alarming rate. If you take two years to finish your book, someone with completely different tastes may be in the chair.

It's up to you to keep yourself informed in every way that may be of help to you in your quest for publication. Subscribe to a writer's magazine; cultivate an acquaintance with your local librarians: ask them for publishers' catalogues; browse through *The Bookseller*, *The Writers' Handbook*, and the *Writers' and Artists' Yearbook*. You'll find a list of other useful books in the appendix.

So, having discovered the perfect setting for your diamond, having created your gem, hewn it from thin air by the sweat of your brow, having worked it, honed it, chipped away at it to make it the right size, reworked it, cursed it, sung about it, wept over it, decided it was brilliant, known it was abysmal . . . at last dawns the day when it's as well cut and brightly polished as you can make it. Now, since it's a manuscript, not a diamond, you have to type the final draft, or send it to a typist, or instruct your computer in the style you wish to print. The last hurdle . . .

Presentation and packaging

First impressions are vital. Too many hopeful writers send off work that, even at first glance, invites an editor to reject it. 'He can't have read it!' you wail when your masterpiece comes back by return of post. But why should he waste his time reading an entire book, or even the brief pages of a short story, when, as soon as he opened the envelope, he knew he was looking at unpublishable work?

'How could he tell, without reading it?'

His first clue could have been the faint, near illegible print, which tells him you hadn't even the courtesy to use a fresh ribbon to save him from eye-strain. How would *you* feel, on a bleak Monday morning, receiving yet another badly presented typescript to add to the pile that was already making your desk, and you, groan with despair?

But *you* wouldn't make a basic mistake like using a worn-out ribbon, would you? You don't *ever* submit hand-written drafts, on small sheets of pink airmail paper, and add a long letter about how you became inspired to write this piece, which is bound to be a best-seller, if only the stupid editor wasn't too blind and evilly disposed towards new writers to see it. Nor do you say that your books are ten times better than J. J. Jones-Jarvis's, and how *he* ever got to be a best-seller when he writes such awful drivel you will never understand . . .

Don't laugh. You may not do these things, but some hopeful writers do.

Some aspirants go to the other extreme and present their manuscripts like finished books, beautifully printed on both sides of the paper, specially bound in a spiral binder, or even with glued edges . . .

But not you – *you* know better. You *always* use:

one side only, of A4 size white paper (80gsm bank, not thin bond).

You also:

leave ample margins (at least an inch) all round;

double-space all lines;

indent paragraphs four or five spaces;

number pages consecutively and

identify each one in some way with your name and/or title of the piece (in case it's dropped and the pages fly apart);

preface your typescript with a title page showing title, author name, approximate wordage and total number of pages, plus your name and address;

check your spelling and punctuation;

make corrections neatly;

keep your accompanying letter brief and to the point;

enclose an SAE (stamped, self-addressed envelope, large enough to hold the MS) or at least send return postage.

And you **always retype at least the first page or two** when your piece has been out a few times and comes home looking crinkled at the edges.

Of course you do!

Or maybe you don't.

But you should.

If you haven't done your homework, haven't even bothered to find out the basics of the business, do you wonder that your chosen editor immediately suspects that your work will prove equally inexpert?

If you have written a work of genius, careful presentation will only enhance it. If your work is not quite so brilliant, at least it will give a good immediate impression and predispose the editor to look on it with favour.

Please don't tell me about that one miraculous case when a bestseller was discovered hand-written on the back of envelopes. Such exceptions are so rare as to be verging on the dodoesque. And do you honestly believe your work is so excellent that it doesn't need all the help it can get? Why give yourself extra problems from the start? Just follow the above guidelines. Easy.

As for **packaging**, if you're sending a book manuscript, simply put your pages into an envelope file, or two if it's a big book, or possibly send it in the cardboard box your paper came in. The editor may want to read it in bed, or over coffee. He'll want to handle one page at a time, for convenience. So make it easy for him. Put this package in a large, strong manilla envelope. Don't guess the weight: remember you should, for politeness' sake, include return postage, so if you haven't got postal scales then leave the final sealing until you've had the package weighed at the post office.

For short pieces use plain manilla envelopes of A4 or A5 size (with the latter you will have to fold the pages in half, which is fine if there are not too many). Use a paper clip to fasten pages together – just a simple paper clip, *not* a staple, *not* a ring-file, or any other of those fancy holders you see in office equipment shops. Be plain. Be professional.

Address it clearly, and add your own name and address on the back in case of problems.

While waiting . . .

Once your MS is in the post, forget about it. You're in for a long wait, probably months, so you might as well be writing your next piece. When I tell people that I wrote five full-length novels before being accepted, they cry, 'How could you keep going?' The secret, dear reader, is persistence. With the first in the post, you work on the next, and when number one returns like a homing pigeon every time you send it out, you have hopes for number two, and when that's in the post you start on number three. Never assume that your first effort is bound to find a publisher eventually. It may do: I hope it does. More likely it's just the first of many that you will pen as you improve your skills.

Even if a publisher is interested, you may have a long wait. If your work is unsolicited, two or three readers may need to give the nod before a proper editor actually looks at your work; only then does it enter the next stages towards acceptance. Decisions involve many people within a company: after editors come sales people, rights departments, production teams and, not least, the ones who hold the purse strings and write those vital cheques: all have to be consulted and satisfied that the product is viable. If you want to include illustrations, artwork or photographs, production costs will mount and accountants may start shaking their heads. In some cases international contacts may need to be consulted before a final offer can be made.

Don't forget that magazine editors work months ahead. If you send them a Christmas piece in October, it may return to you only because at the moment they're planning their spring issues.

This being so, you will appreciate the need for patience. Don't start harassing your publisher after only a week or two. If you're anxious to be sure your work has arrived, you might enclose a card already made out with message and bearing your name, address and a stamp; the publisher can slip it into the post as an acknowledgement. As I've said before, he can't take the time to write back to every hopeful author. Slush piles (that is, stacks of manuscripts that arrive uninvited) are vast, and yours is just another envelope among hundreds. If you haven't heard anything after six months or so, you might write a polite query letter to remind them you exist.

Accepted! Hooray!

At last comes the letter of acceptance, stating how much they're offering for your gem. For a book, this will probably be an advance against royalties. Oh, frabjous day! But, on second glance, the amount may look pretty small compared with all those six-figure numbers you've heard bandied about. Truth is, fortunes are rarely made overnight. If you're in this for the money you might as well save time by doing the pools, or buying lottery tickets.

Not long ago, the Society of Authors did a survey of its members. The result showed that of those British authors who answered the questionnaire one per cent were making a pretty good living, thank you. Ninety-five per cent earned less than £500 a year from their pens. The other four per cent were somewhere in between.

So, even if your piece should be accepted, don't give up the day job.

Rejected! Gloom, despair, depression . . .

If, after everything, your work is rejected, don't despair. Many a bestseller has been turned down by a dozen or more publishers before finding its eventual home. Publishing often comes down to personal taste and if your work happens to fit the preference of a particular editor it has a good chance; if it doesn't appeal to him, another editor may love it. So, choose another *suitable* market and put your MS back in the post. If necessary, especially with a short piece, rewrite it a little to suit its new destination. There are scores of magazines out there, and in 1994 an amazing 900 UK publishers exhibited at the Frankfurt Book Fair. This gives you ample scope for continued hope.

And always, always, be working on something new. That first piece may never find a publisher. Be honest with yourself, look at it again a few years on. Now that you're a better writer, you can probably see what rubbish that early effort is. You should see some of my tyro stories!

I should like to state that if your work has any merit at all it's bound to find a publisher sooner or later, but the publishing world has to balance its books and even if your writing is excellent it may not be commercial. If all else fails and you still think your words are worth a wider audience, you might think of becoming your own publisher.

Self-publishing – a possibility

If your book has a limited audience, say something of interest mainly in your own locality, or perhaps a book of poems, a very short book on a hobby subject, or if you simply *must* see it in print and no one else will do it, then self-publishing is an option. This means finding a friendly printer with whom you collaborate in the production and with whom you share the costs and the profits (if any). Exact terms would depend on questions such as length of book, whether illustrations/photos are needed, what kind of cover it has, and so on. Expect to spend several hundred pounds, minimum.

Apart from the financial cost, allow also for the time it will take, first in planning and organization, then in distributing and selling the book: this chore will fall on you, too, if you hope to recoup any of your outlay. It *has* been known for such books to become so popular that a commercial publisher takes them up, but don't count on that happening as it's a rare occurrence. Think very, very carefully before you embark on self-publishing. Be absolutely sure you're doing it for the right reasons and that you can afford to take the chance.

If you do decide to go ahead, take special care with your editing, and if possible find a professional to help you. So many self-published books, crammed with fascinating facts and insights, are spoiled by being badly put together, retaining many of the basic faults I've been listing in this book. Is this the reason your work has been turned down by commercial publishers? Do you really want to send it out badly written and looking like the work of a rank amateur, with *your* name proudly blazoned on the cover? For your own sake, take advice before you do such a thing. If you want to be a published writer then do it properly, professionally.

Vanity publishing – be warned

A lady once asked me how much it cost me to have my books published; she was astounded when I replied that publishers paid *me*. If you're not yet in this fortunate situation, and if you don't fancy the expense and effort involved in self-publishing, please beware of unscrupulous people – so-called 'vanity publishers' – who will tell you your work is wonderful and offer to produce it in return for large sums of money. DON'T BE TAKEN IN. You may find yourself with a house full of cheap and nasty books that nobody will buy. Your 'publisher' won't help you to sell them, won't make an effort at publicity, won't want to hear your complaints: he's out to make money – *your* money – out of *your* desperate desire to see yourself in print whatever the cost. Long queues of disillusioned writers are waiting to get their money back from such sharks.

Nil desperandum

When your spirits are at their lowest ebb, remember that there *are* a lot of people out there getting published every day. You *can* be one of them, if you want it enough to work at it. You may never earn a fortune, but what a joy to see your name in print in a magazine, or emblazoned on the spine of a book.

If nothing else, writing is an enjoyable and fulfilling hobby. You don't need a university degree; you don't need expensive equipment, or special clothing; you don't even need good health and lots of energy. Anybody can do it, whatever their circumstances, whatever their age. If you can't write for publication, you can write for your family, or for your friends. But, most of all, write for yourself, because you love it, because your life would be empty without it. That's why I began (aged eight) and what kept me going long before my work saw print, and what will keep me going for as long as I'm capable of writing. Just putting words on paper. A lovely pastime. Cheap, non-fattening, fun . . . Enjoy it.

All power to your pen!

Appendix I

For your reference shelf

If you don't already possess them, acquire as many of the following as you can:

A good dictionary

A spelling dictionary

A thesaurus

The Oxford Dictionary for Writers and Editors

Any other type of dictionary you think might be useful: Collins Gem series is inexpensive and handy to use.

The Complete Plain Words, Sir Ernest Gowers

Mind the Stop: A Brief Guide to Punctuation, G. V. Carey

Other grammar reference books

The Writers' and Artists' Yearbook or *The Writer's Handbook* – updated annually, both contain much useful information, including details of many markets for your work. (If you can't obtain a copy for your own use, your library's reference section should have one.)

Pears Cyclopaedia, crammed with basic information on many topics

A book of quotations

Good general reference books

Reference books on any subject. Become a collector, especially when browsing at jumble and car boot sales.

History, costume, transport, travel, wartime, true-life stories . . . whatever suits your needs.

Publishers' pamphlets on 'house style'

Not least, collect books on writing – as many as you can. Every writer has a slightly different view to offer.

Appendix II

Suggested Answers
From Chapter Seven:
Change examples from reported to direct speech:

1. The driver addressed me abruptly, asking if I was from Lynn.

   'You from Lynn?' the driver asked. (His words imply the abruptness, so the adverb can be left out.)

2. She enquired, rather sarcastically, if he was aware how much phone calls cost these days.

   'I suppose you're blissfully unaware how much phone calls cost these days?' she said. (The rewording implies the sarcasm.)

3. Max queried the meaning of the word 'scatty'.

   '"Scatty"?' Max queried. OR *'What does "scatty" mean?' Max asked.*

4. As he opened the car door, he told her to move over.

   'Move over,' he said as he opened the car door.

5. Roughly, Carl said she should stop being so stupid.

   'Stop being so stupid!' Carl snarled. (Use a strong verb – 'snarled' rather than 'said roughly'.)

6. 'So he says,' Mrs Turnip gossiped, '"Annie wouldn't have done that," he says. So I says, "Blast, and she would!" And so she would!'

7. He insisted on putting the car into the barn for me, so I got out and directed him into the narrow space.

(The last two examples are, I suggest, best left as they are because:

6. shows how she talks and puts her in character.

7. If this were put into direct speech it would take up too much space for such a trivial exchange.)

Note that direct speech is much more vivid but, because it needs more space, be sure it's relevant i.e. it must advance the plot, reveal character and/or raise questions in the reader's mind.

From Chapter Eleven

One way of activating that passive passage:

On a misty, golden morning, the trees all wore the same green uniform, some turning brown at the cuffs, and in hedgerows black-berries hung in thick clusters. As Mike cycled into the vale, laughter sounded from a field where women gleaned among corn stubble, while on the opposite side of the road men harvested runner beans.

Two heavy horses in tandem clopped up from the village, pulling a threshing machine, and by a cottage gate a woman ladled milk from her cycle-cart into a great blue jug held by an urchin in over-sized cap and baggy shorts. His mother shouted instructions to him from the end of the path, where she stood with a baby on her hip.

Remember, though, that if this were in a story, it would need to include extra elements, such as some pertinent dialogue or glimpses of Mike's thoughts, so as not to halt the action of the story.